T0358251

About This Book

Why This Book Is Important

This fourth book in the M&E Series explains a critical step of the ROI Methodology: converting impact data to monetary values. After isolating the effects of a program, the only way to understand the true impact of a program is to determine the monetary value of the business impact. This book examines the different techniques for translating data into monetary terms.

Although executives want to see the monetary value of programs, other benefits occur that we often choose not to convert to monetary values; these are intangible benefits. This book explains intangible measures and why they are important. These intangible benefits are often as important to some organizations as monetary benefits.

What This Book Achieves

This book shows how to convert impact data to monetary values by means of the following techniques:

- Using standard values

- Calculating the value

- Consulting sources in order to find the value

- Estimating the value

The book also explains how to select the appropriate technique for any situation and any level of evaluation.

How This Book Is Organized

This book introduces and describes the techniques that can be used to convert data to monetary values and ends by discussing the methods that are best for each situation. It begins with a brief introduction to the ROI process model and the Twelve Guiding Principles of the ROI Methodology. Chapter One discusses why data conversion is important. Converting data to monetary values helps executives see the value of programs and projects in terms that they understand. The first chapter also examines the different kinds of data and the steps that must be taken to convert each type to a monetary value.

The remainder of the book explains the techniques that can be used to convert data to monetary values. Chapter Two details the use of standard values that have been developed by others who measured the same items. This is the most credible technique for data conversion. This chapter explains why standard values have been developed and provides some examples of standard values. Chapter Three discusses the many ways in which monetary values can be calculated—for example, by using historical costs or by linking the data with other measures.

Chapter Four describes how to locate sources of monetary values, such as internal and external experts and external databases. Chapter Five illustrates how estimates can be used to convert impact data to monetary values. Estimates, the least credible technique, can be obtained from program participants, participants' supervisors and managers, or program staff.

Chapter Six explains how to select the appropriate technique, ensure accuracy and credibility, and make adjustments in order to improve credibility. At the end of the chapter, a matching exercise tests the reader on how to select the correct technique for a given situation. Finally, Chapter Seven discusses why intangible measures are important. It also examines how to decide whether to convert intangible measures to money.

The Measurement and Evaluation Series

Editors

Patricia Pulliam Phillips, Ph.D.

Jack J. Phillips, Ph.D.

Introduction to the Measurement and Evaluation Series

The ROI Six Pack provides detailed information on developing ROI evaluations, implementing the ROI Methodology, and showing the value of a variety of functions and processes. With detailed examples, tools, templates, shortcuts, and checklists, this series will be a valuable reference for individuals interested in using the ROI Methodology to show the impact of their projects, programs, and processes.

The Need

Although financial ROI has been measured for over one hundred years to quantify the value of plants, equipment, and companies, the concept has only recently been applied to evaluate the impact of learning and development, human resources, technology, quality, marketing, and other support functions. In the learning and development field alone, the use of ROI has become routine in many organizations. In the past decade, hundreds of organizations have embraced the ROI process to show the impact of many different projects and programs.

Along the way, professionals and practitioners need help. They need tools, templates, and tips, along with explanations, examples, and details, to make this process work. Without this help, using the ROI Methodology to show the value of projects and programs is difficult. In short, practitioners need shortcuts and proven techniques to minimize the resources required to use this process. Practitioners' needs have created the need for this series. This series will provide the detail necessary to make the ROI Methodology successful within an organization. For easy reference and use, the books are logically arranged to align with the steps of the ROI Methodology.

Audience

The principal audience for these books is individuals who plan to use the ROI Methodology to show the value of their projects and programs. Such individuals are specialists or managers charged with proving the value of their particular project or program. They need detailed information, know-how, and confidence.

A second audience is those who have used the ROI Methodology for some time but want a quick reference with tips and techniques to make ROI implementation more successful within their organization. This series, which explains the evaluation process in detail, will be a valuable reference set for these individuals, regardless of other ROI publications owned.

A third audience is consultants and researchers who want to know how to address specific evaluation issues. Three important challenges face individuals as they measure ROI and conduct ROI evaluations: (1) collecting post-program data, (2) isolating the effects of the program, and (3) converting data to monetary values. A book is devoted to each of these critical issues, allowing researchers and consultants to easily find details on each issue.

A fourth audience is those who are curious about the ROI Methodology and its use. The first book in this series focuses specifically on ROI, its use, and how to determine whether it is appropriate for an organization. When interest is piqued, the remaining books provide more detail.

Flow of the Books

The six books are presented in a logical sequence, mirroring the ROI process model. Book one, *ROI Fundamentals: Why and When to Measure ROI*, presents the basic ROI Methodology and makes the business case for measuring ROI as it explores the benefits and barriers to implementation. It also examines the type of organization best suited for the ROI Methodology and the best time to implement it. Planning for an ROI evaluation is also explored in this book.

Book two, *Data Collection: Planning For and Collecting All Types of Data*, details data collection by examining the different techniques, methods, and issues involved in this process, with an emphasis on collecting post-program data. It examines the different data collection methods: questionnaires, interviews, focus groups, observation, action plans, performance contracts, and monitoring records.

Book three, *Isolation of Results: Defining the Impact of the Program*, focuses on the most valuable part of the ROI Methodology and the essential step for ensuring credibility. Recognizing that factors other than the program being measured can influence results, this book shows a variety of ways in which the effects of a program can be isolated from other influences. Techniques include comparison analysis using a control group, trend line analysis and forecasting methods, and expert input from a variety of sources.

Book four, *Data Conversion: Calculating the Monetary Benefits*, covers perhaps the second toughest challenge of ROI evaluation: placing monetary value on program benefits. To calculate the ROI, data must be converted to money, and *Data Conversion* shows how this conversion has been accomplished in a variety of organizations. The good news is that standard values are available for many items. When they are not, the book shows different techniques for converting them, ranging from calculating the value from records to seeking experts and searching databases. When data cannot be converted to money credibly and with minimum resources, they are considered intangible. This book explores the range of intangible benefits and the necessary techniques for collecting, analyzing, and recording them.

Book five, *Costs and ROI: Evaluating at the Ultimate Level*, focuses on costs and ROI. This book shows that all costs must be captured in order to create a fully loaded cost profile. All the costs must be included in order to be conservative and to give the analysis additional credibility. Next, the actual ROI calculation is presented, showing the various assumptions and issues that must be addressed when calculating the ROI. Three different calculations are presented: the benefit-cost ratio, the ROI percentage, and the payback period. The book concludes with several cautions and concerns about the use of ROI and its meaning.

Book six, *Communication and Implementation: Sustaining the Practice*, explores two important issues. The first issue is reporting the results of an evaluation. This is the final part of the ROI Methodology and is necessary to ensure that audiences have the information they need so that improvement processes can be implemented. A range of techniques is available, including face-to-face meetings, brief reports, one-page summaries, routine communications, mass-audience techniques, and electronic media. All are available for reporting evaluation results. The final part of the book focuses on how to sustain the ROI evaluation process: how to use it, keep it going, and make it work in the long term to add value to the organization and, often, to show the value of all the programs and projects within a function or department.

Terminology: Programs, Projects, Solutions

In this series the terms *program* and *project* are used to describe many processes that can be evaluated using the ROI Methodology. This is an important issue because readers may vary widely in their perspectives. Individuals involved in technology applications may

Table I.1. Terms and Applications

Term	Example
Program	Leadership development skills enhancement for senior executives
Project	A reengineering scheme for a plastics division
System	A fully interconnected network for all branches of a bank
Initiative	A faith-based effort to reduce recidivism
Policy	A new preschool plan for disadvantaged citizens
Procedure	A new scheduling arrangement for truck drivers
Event	A golf outing for customers
Meeting	A U.S. Coast Guard conference on innovations
Process	Quality sampling
People	Staff additions in the customer care center
Tool	A new means of selecting hotel staff

use the terms *system* and *technology* rather than *program* or *project*. In public policy, in contrast, the word *program* is prominent. For a professional meetings and events planner, the word *program* may not be pertinent, but in human resources, *program* is often used. Finding one term for all these situations would be difficult. Consequently, the terms *program* and *project* are used interchangeably. Table I.1 lists these and other terms that may be used in other contexts.

Features

Each book in the series takes a straightforward approach to make it understandable, practical, and useful. Checklists are provided, charts are included, templates are presented, and examples are explored. All are intended to show how the ROI Methodology works. The focus of these books is implementing the process and making it successful within an organization. The methodology is based on the work of hundreds of individuals who have made the ROI Methodology a successful evaluation process within their organizations.

About Pfeiffer

Pfeiffer serves the professional development and hands-on resource needs of training and human resource practitioners and gives them products to do their jobs better. We deliver proven ideas and solutions from experts in HR development and HR management, and we offer effective and customizable tools to improve workplace performance. From novice to seasoned professional, Pfeiffer is the source you can trust to make yourself and your organization more successful.

Essential Knowledge Pfeiffer produces insightful, practical, and comprehensive materials on topics that matter the most to training and HR professionals. Our Essential Knowledge resources translate the expertise of seasoned professionals into practical, how-to guidance on critical workplace issues and problems. These resources are supported by case studies, worksheets, and job aids and are frequently supplemented with CD-ROMs, Web sites, and other means of making the content easier to read, understand, and use.

Essential Tools Pfeiffer's Essential Tools resources save time and expense by offering proven, ready-to-use materials—including exercises, activities, games, instruments, and assessments—for use during a training or team-learning event. These resources are frequently offered in looseleaf or CD-ROM format to facilitate copying and customization of the material.

Pfeiffer also recognizes the remarkable power of new technologies in expanding the reach and effectiveness of training. While e-hype has often created whizbang solutions in search of a problem, we are dedicated to bringing convenience and enhancements to proven training solutions. All our e-tools comply with rigorous functionality standards. The most appropriate technology wrapped around essential content yields the perfect solution for today's on-the-go trainers and human resource professionals.

Pfeiffer *Essential resources for training and HR professionals*
www.pfeiffer.com

Data Conversion

Calculating the Monetary Benefits

Patricia Pulliam Phillips, Ph.D.
Holly Burkett, M.A.

Pfeiffer

A Wiley Imprint
www.pfeiffer.com

Published by Pfeiffer
An Imprint of Wiley
989 Market Street, San Francisco, CA 94103-1741
www.pfeiffer.com

For additional copies/bulk purchases of this book in the U.S. please contact 800-274-4434.

Pfeiffer books and products are available through most bookstores. To contact Pfeiffer directly call our Customer Care Department within the U.S. at 800-274-4434, outside the U.S. at 317-572-3985, fax 317-572-4002, or visit www.pfeiffer.com.

Pfeiffer also publishes its books in a variety of electronic formats. Some content that appears in print may not be available in electronic books.

Library of Congress Cataloging-in-Publication Data

Phillips, Patricia Pulliam.
   Data conversion: calculating the monetary benefits / Patricia Pulliam Phillips, Holly Burkett.
      p.   cm.
   Includes bibliographical references and index.
   ISBN 978-0-7879-8720-6 (pbk.)
      1. Project management—Cost effectiveness.   2. Rate of return.   3. Activity-based costing.   4. Project management—Evaluation.   I. Burkett, Holly.   II. Title.
   HD69.P75.P4962   2008
   658.15'54—dc22

                                                                        2007045002

Production Editor: Michael Kay   Editorial Assistant: Julie Rodriguez
Editor: Matthew Davis   Manufacturing Supervisor: Becky Morgan
Printed in the United States of America

PB Printing 10 9 8 7 6 5 4 3 2 1

Contents

Acknowledgments from the Editors

From Patti

No project, regardless of its size or scope, is completed without the help and support of others. My sincere thanks go to the staff at Pfeiffer. Their support for this project has been relentless. Matt Davis has been the greatest! It is our pleasure and privilege to work with such a professional and creative group of people.

Thanks also go to my husband, Jack. His unwavering support of my work is always evident. His idea for the series was to provide readers with a practical understanding of the various components of a comprehensive measurement and evaluation process. Thank you, Jack, for another fun opportunity!

From Jack

Many thanks go to the staff who helped make this series a reality. Lori Ditoro did an excellent job of meeting a very tight deadline and delivering a quality manuscript.

Much admiration and thanks go to Patti. She is an astute observer of the ROI Methodology, having observed and learned from hundreds of presentations, consulting assignments, and engagements. In addition, she is an excellent researcher and student of the process, studying how it is developed and how it works. She has become an ROI expert in her own right. Thanks, Patti, for your many contributions. You are a great partner, friend, and spouse.

Principles of the ROI Methodology

The ROI Methodology is a step-by-step tool for evaluating any program, project, or initiative in any organization. Figure P.1 illustrates the ROI process model, which makes a potentially complicated process simple by breaking it into sequential steps. The ROI process model provides a systematic, step-by-step approach to ROI evaluations that helps keep the process manageable, allowing users to address one issue at a time. The model also emphasizes that the ROI Methodology is a logical, systematic process that flows from one step to another and provides a way for evaluators to collect and analyze six types of data.

Applying the model consistently from one program to another is essential for successful evaluation. To aid consistent application of the model, the ROI Methodology is based on twelve Guiding Principles. These principles are necessary for a credible, conservative approach to evaluation through the different levels.

1. When conducting a higher-level evaluation, collect data at lower levels.

2. When planning a higher-level evaluation, the previous level of evaluation is not required to be comprehensive.

3. When collecting and analyzing data, use only the most credible sources.

Figure P.1. The ROI Process Model

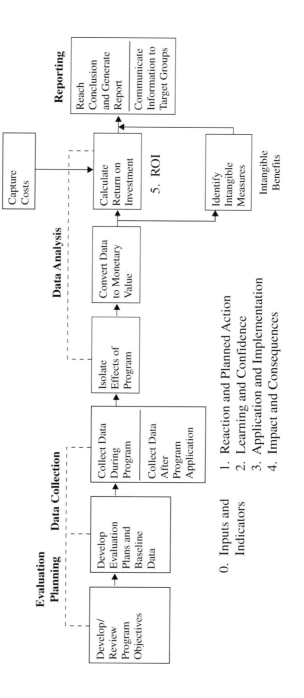

Evaluation Planning   **Data Collection**   **Data Analysis**   **Reporting**

Develop/Review Program Objectives

Develop Evaluation Plans and Baseline Data

Collect Data During Program / Collect Data After Program Application

Isolate Effects of Program

Convert Data to Monetary Value

Capture Costs

Calculate Return on Investment

5. ROI

Identify Intangible Measures

Intangible Benefits

Reach Conclusion and Generate Report / Communicate Information to Target Groups

0. Inputs and Indicators
1. Reaction and Planned Action
2. Learning and Confidence
3. Application and Implementation
4. Impact and Consequences

4. When analyzing data, select the most conservative alternative for calculations.

5. Use at least one method to isolate the effects of a project.

6. If no improvement data are available for a population or from a specific source, assume that little or no improvement has occurred.

7. Adjust estimates of improvement for potential errors of estimation.

8. Avoid use of extreme data items and unsupported claims when calculating ROI.

9. Use only the first year of annual benefits in ROI analysis of short-term solutions.

10. Fully load all costs of a solution, project, or program when analyzing ROI.

11. Intangible measures are defined as measures that are purposely not converted to monetary values.

12. Communicate the results of the ROI Methodology to all key stakeholders.

The Importance of Converting Data to Monetary Values

Traditionally, most impact evaluation studies stop with a tabulation of business results. In these situations, the program is considered successful if it produced improvements such as productivity increases, quality enhancements, absenteeism reductions, or customer satisfaction improvements. While these results are important, converting the data to monetary values and showing the total monetary impact of the improvement provides more concrete data for determining and validating program success. This calculation responds to the request "Show me the money." Also, the monetary value of program benefits is needed for comparison with the cost of the program in developing the return on investment (ROI). This evaluation is the ultimate level of the evaluation framework on which the ROI Methodology is based.

This book shows how leading organizations are moving beyond simply tabulating business results and are adding the step of converting data to monetary values.

This initial chapter focuses on the importance of taking this extra step. It also explores some of the preliminary issues that must be considered before addressing the specific techniques available for converting data to money.

Why Convert Data to Monetary Values?

The need to convert data to monetary amounts is not always clearly understood. A program or project can be shown to be a success just by providing business impact data showing the amount of change directly attributable to the program. For example, a change in quality, cycle time, market share, or customer satisfaction could represent a significant improvement linked directly to a new program. For some programs, this may be sufficient. However, many sponsors require the actual monetary value, and increasingly, evaluators are taking the extra step of converting data to monetary values.

Value Equals Money

For some stakeholders, the most important value is money. Although there are many different types of value, monetary value is one of the primary criteria of success. Executives, sponsors, clients, administrators, and other leaders are concerned with the allocation of funds and want to see evidence of the contribution of a program in terms of monetary value. Often, for these key stakeholders, outcomes stated in any other terms are unsatisfactory.

Impact Is More Understandable

For some programs, the impact is more understandable when it is stated in terms of monetary value. Consider, for example, the impact of a major program to improve the creativity of an organization's employees and thereby enhance the innovation of the organization. Suppose this program involved all employees and had an impact on all parts of the organization. Across all departments, functions, units, and divisions, employees were being more creative, suggesting new ideas, taking on new challenges, driving new products—in short, helping the organization in a wide variety of ways. The easiest way to understand the value of such a program is to convert the individual efforts and their consequences to monetary values. Totaling the monetary values of all the innovations can provide a sense of the value of the program.

Consider the impact of a leadership development program directed at all of the middle managers in an organization. As part of the program, the managers were asked to select at least two measures of importance to them and to indicate what would need to change or improve for them to meet their specific goals. The measures numbered in the dozens. When the program's impact was studied, a large number of improvements were identified but were hard to quantify. Converting them to monetary values allowed these improvements to be expressed in the same terms, enabling the outcomes to be more clearly reported.

As described in earlier books in this series, the monetary value of program benefits is needed to compare against costs in order to develop the benefit-cost ratio, the ROI (as a percentage), and the payback period. Calculating ROI is impossible without converting data to monetary amounts.

Programs Start Because of Money

Sometimes, the monetary value of a particular issue provides the impetus for a program. For example, a company might be experiencing huge fines due to compliance violations, and these fines result in a program to prevent further violations. In another example, excessive accidents, when converted to monetary values, might illustrate the magnitude of a problem, which leads directly to new programs to lower the number of accidents. Essentially, the best way to get the attention of a potential sponsor for a program is to place the problem or opportunity in the context of money. This almost guarantees that the program will be implemented, if the data are credible and the resources are available.

Converting Data to Money Is Similar to Budgeting

Professionals and administrators work with budgets and are expected to develop budgets for programs with an acceptable degree of accuracy; thus they are comfortable with tabulating costs. When it comes to benefits, however, many are not comfortable, even though some of the same techniques used to develop budgets are used to determine benefits. Defining the benefits of a program in terms of cost savings or cost reductions may make identification of the costs or value of the program easier for some managers. The monetary benefit resulting from a program becomes a natural extension of the budget.

Monetary Value Is Vital to Organizational Operations

With global competitiveness and the drive to improve the efficiency of operations, awareness of the costs related to particular processes and activities is essential. In the 1990s, this emphasis gave rise to activity-based costing (ABC) and activity-based management. ABC is not a replacement for traditional general ledger accounting. Rather, it is a translator or medium between cost accumulations—that is, the specific expenditure account balances in the general ledger—and the end users who must apply cost data in decision making. In typical cost statements, the actual cost of a process or problem is not readily discernible. ABC converts inert cost data to relevant, actionable information. ABC has become increasingly useful for identifying improvement opportunities and measuring the benefits realized from performance initiatives (Cokins, 1996). Over 80 percent of the ROI impact studies that have been conducted show that a program has benefited an organization through cost savings (cost reduction or cost avoidance). Understanding the cost of a problem and the payoff of the corresponding solution is essential to proper management of a business.

Monetary Values Are Necessary to Understand Problems

In any business, costs are essential to understanding the magnitude of a problem. Consider, for example, the cost of employee turnover. Traditional records and even those available through activity-based costing will not indicate the full cost of the problem. A variety of estimates and expert inputs may be necessary to supplement cost statements in order to arrive at a specific value. The good news is that organizations have developed a number of standard procedures for identifying undesirable costs. For example, Wal-Mart has calculated the cost of one truck sitting idle at a store for one minute, waiting to be unloaded. When this cost is multiplied by hundreds of deliveries per store and then multiplied by five thousand stores, the cost becomes enormous. Understanding the enormity of the cost gives the retailer an undisputable reason why strides must be taken to ensure the trucks are unloaded as quickly as possible.

Hard and Soft Data

When collecting business impact data, some managers find it helpful to divide the data into two categories: hard data and soft data. Hard data are obtained through the traditional measures of organizational performance. Hard data are objective, easy to measure, and easy to convert to monetary values. Because hard data are often obtained through common performance measures, they enjoy high credibility with management and are available in almost every organization. They are destined to be converted to monetary values and included in the ROI calculation.

Hard data represent the output, quality, cost, and time of work-related processes. Table 1.1 shows examples of data in these four categories. Almost every department or function will have performance measures that yield hard data. For example, a government

Table 1.1. Examples of Hard Data

Output	Quality	Cost	Time
Units produced	Failure rates	Shelter costs	Cycle time
Tons manufactured	Dropout rates	Treatment costs	Equipment downtime
Items assembled	Scrap	Budget variances	Overtime
Money collected	Waste	Unit costs	On-time shipments
Items sold	Rejects	Cost by account	Time to project completion
New accounts generated	Error rates	Variable costs	Processing time
Forms processed	Rework	Fixed costs	Supervisory time
Loans approved	Shortages	Overhead cost	Time to proficiency
Inventory turnover	Product defects	Operating costs	Learning time
Patients visited	Deviation from standard	Program cost savings	Adherence to schedules
Applications processed	Product failures	Accident costs	Repair time
Students graduated	Inventory adjustments	Program costs	Efficiency
Tasks completed	Time card corrections	Sales expense	Work stoppages
Output per hour	Incidents		Order response time
Productivity	Compliance discrepancies		Late reporting
Work backlog	Agency fines		Lost-time days
Incentive bonus			
Shipments			
Completion rate			

office that approves applications for work visas might track the following four performance measures: number of applications processed (output), number of errors made in processing applications (quality), cost per application processed (cost), and average time taken to process and approve an application (time). Most projects or programs in this unit should be linked to one or more hard data measures.

Because many programs are designed to develop soft skills, soft data must also be collected during evaluation. Soft data are usually subjective, are sometimes difficult to measure, are almost always difficult to convert to monetary values, and are behavior-oriented. Compared with hard data, soft data are usually perceived as less credible although we use them frequently when managing organization processes. Soft data measures may or may not be converted to monetary values.

Soft data items can be grouped into several categories; Table 1.2 shows one such grouping. Measures such as employee complaints and grievances are listed as soft data items not because they are difficult to measure but because they are difficult to convert accurately to monetary values.

Converting Data to Monetary Values

Before describing the techniques to convert either hard or soft data to monetary values, we will briefly summarize the steps used to convert data in each category. These steps should be followed each time a measure is converted to monetary value.

1. Focus on a Unit of Measure

First, identify a unit of measure targeted for improvement. For output data, the unit of measure might be an item produced, a service provided, or a sale completed. Time measures are varied and include items such as the time to complete a program, cycle time, or customer response time. Units of time measures are usually

Table 1.2. Examples of Soft Data

Work Habits
- Excessive breaks
- Tardiness
- Visits to the dispensary
- Violations of safety rules
- Communication
- breakdowns

Work Climate and Job Satisfaction
- Grievances
- Discrimination charges
- Employee complaints
- Job satisfaction
- Employee organizational commitment
- Employee engagement
- Employee loyalty
- Intent to leave the organization
- Stress

Initiative and Innovation
- Creativity
- Innovation
- New ideas
- Suggestions
- New products and services
- Trademarks
- Copyrights and patents
- Process improvements
- Partnerships and alliances

Customer Service
- Customer complaints
- Customer satisfaction
- Customer dissatisfaction
- Customer impressions
- Customer loyalty
- Customer retention
- Lost customers

Employee Development and Advancement
- Promotions
- Capability
- Intellectual capital
- Requests for transfer
- Performance appraisal ratings
- Readiness
- Networking

Image
- Brand awareness
- Reputation
- Leadership
- Social responsibility
- Environmental friendliness
- Social consciousness
- Diversity
- External awards

expressed in minutes, hours, or days. For quality the unit might be one error, reject, defect, or rework item. Soft data measures are varied; a unit of improvement might be one sale or a change of one point in the employee engagement score. Here are some specific examples of units of improvement:

- One student enrolled
- One patient served
- One loan approved
- One full-time employee hired
- One reworked item
- One grievance
- One voluntary turnover
- One hour of downtime
- One hour of cycle time
- One hour of employee time
- One customer complaint
- One person removed from welfare
- One less day of incarceration (prison)
- One point increase in customer satisfaction

2. Determine the Value of Each Unit

Now, the challenge: place a value (V) on the unit of measure identified in the first step. This step is the focus of this book. For measures of production, quality, cost, and time, this process is relatively easy. Most organizations have records or reports that state the value of items such as one unit of production or the cost of a defect. Soft data are more difficult to convert to a value; the cost of one absence, one grievance, or a change of one point in the employee attitude survey is often difficult to pinpoint. The techniques in this book provide an array of possibilities for making this conversion. When more than one value is available, either the most credible or the lowest value is used.

3. Calculate the Change in Performance

The change in output data is calculated after the effects of the program have been isolated from other influences. The change (Δ) is the performance improvement, expressed in hard or soft data, which is directly attributable to the program. The value may represent the performance improvement for an individual, a team, a group, or several groups of participants.

4. Determine the Annual Amount of Change

Annualize the value by calculating the total change in the performance data that would occur in one year if improvement were to continue at the same rate that was recorded during the program (ΔP). In many organizations, calculating the benefits for one year has become a standard approach to defining the total benefits of a program. Although the benefits may not be realized at the same level for an entire year, some programs will continue to produce benefits beyond one year. In some cases, the stream of benefits may continue for several years. Using one year of benefits is considered a conservative approach, leading to Guiding Principle 9: Use only the first year of annual benefits in ROI analysis of short-term solutions.

5. Calculate the Total Value of the Improvement

Compute the total value of improvement that can be attributed to the program by multiplying the unit value (V) by the annual performance change (ΔP). For example, if a group of fifteen supervisors attended a program designed to reduce the number of complaints filed by a specific employee group, the annual change in performance would be the total number by which grievances were reduced for the entire year, not just up to the point in time at which the data were collected. This annual improvement is then multiplied by the value of one unit to calculate the total monetary benefits to the organization.

Another example of this calculation is annualizing the measure representative of a large population. If a group of twenty managers attended a program designed to reduce absenteeism, the annualized performance change would reflect the reduction in absenteeism for the entire target population (say two hundred employees working in operations) over the course of one year. This value is then multiplied by the unit value of one absence to calculate the annual monetary benefits of the program. This value for the total annual program benefits is then compared with the cost of the program, usually by using the return on investment formula presented in *ROI Fundamentals*, the first book of this series.

Case Example of Converting Data to Monetary Values

An example taken from a team-building program at a manufacturing plant illustrates the five-step process of converting data to monetary values. This program was developed and implemented after a needs assessment revealed that lack of teamwork was causing an excessive number of grievances. The number of grievances resolved at step 2 in the four-step grievance process was selected as an impact measure. Exhibit 1.1 shows the steps taken to assign monetary values to the reduction in grievances.

Final Thoughts

This brief chapter sets the stage for addressing one of the critical issues in an ROI evaluation: converting data to monetary values. This chapter shows the rationale for this step and some of the key issues that must be addressed when beginning the process.

As this book will illustrate, many techniques can be used to convert data to monetary values; the good news is that often much of the conversion work has already been done. Several techniques are available for converting data to monetary values. Some methods are appropriate only for a specific type of data, while others can be used with virtually any type of data. The challenge is to select the

Exhibit 1.1. Converting Data to Monetary Values: Evaluation of a Team-Building Program in a Manufacturing Plant

Step 1:	**Define the unit of measure.**
	Unit of measure = one less grievance reaching step 2 in the four-step grievance resolution process.
Step 2:	**Determine the value of each unit.**
	Using internal experts on the labor relations staff, the cost of an average grievance was estimated to be $6,500, considering time and direct costs. ($V = \$6,500$)
Step 3:	**Calculate the change in performance.**
	Six months after the program was completed, total grievances per month reaching step 2 had declined by ten. Supervisors isolated the effects of the program, determining that seven of the ten grievance reductions were related to the program. ($\Delta = 7$)
Step 4:	**Determine an annual amount of change.**
	Using the adjusted Δ value of seven per month yields an annual improvement of eighty-four (7 fewer grievances $\times$ 12 months) for the first year. ($\Delta P = 84$)
Step 5:	**Calculate the total value of the improvement.**
	Annual value $= \Delta P \times V$
	$\qquad\qquad = 84 \times \$6,500$
	$\qquad\qquad = \$546,000$

technique that best matches the type of data and situation. Each method is presented in the next four chapters, beginning with the most credible approach. The next chapter focuses on the easiest method for getting to the monetary value: finding standard values that have already been converted.

Reference

Cokins, G. *Activity-Based Cost Management: Making It Work—A Manager's Guide to Implementing and Sustaining an Effective ABC System.* New York: McGraw-Hill, 1996.

2

Use Standard Values

Perhaps the best news about converting data to monetary values is that it has already been done for most of the measures that matter in an organization. It is estimated that 80 percent of the measures that are important to an organization have been converted to monetary values. That is, if it is important enough to drive a program or project, then someone has been concerned enough about it to convert it to a monetary value.

This chapter highlights the progress that has been made in developing standard values. A standard value is defined as a value that is accepted by an organization as the monetary cost or value of a particular unit of measure. This chapter divides the standard values into output, quality, and time—three of the four major categories of hard data that are described in Chapter One.

Converting Output Data to Monetary Values

When a program has produced a change in output, the value of the increased output can be determined from the organization's accounting or operating records. Output measures include revenue and productivity measures. For organizations operating on a profit basis, this value is usually the marginal profit contribution of an additional unit of production or unit of service provided. For example, if a production team in a major appliance manufacturer is able to boost production of small refrigerators with a series of comprehensive programs, the unit of improvement is the profit margin on the sale of one refrigerator. In organizations that are performance-driven rather than profit-driven, the value of increased output is reflected in the savings accumulated when additional output is realized without increasing input requirements. For example, in a university, if an additional student application is processed at no additional cost, the increase in output translates into a cost savings equal to the original unit cost of processing an application.

The formulas and calculations used to measure the value of the increased output depend on the organization and its records. Most organizations have this type of data readily available for use in performance monitoring and goal setting. Managers often use marginal cost statements and sensitivity analyses to pinpoint the value associated with changes in output. If a value for the desired output measure is not available, staff members must initiate or coordinate the development of an appropriate value.

Case Example: A Commercial Bank

In one case involving a commercial bank, a sales seminar for consumer loan officers was conducted, resulting in increased consumer loan volume (output). To measure the return on investment in the program, it was necessary to calculate the value (profit contribution) of one additional consumer loan, which could be calculated rather easily by using data from the bank's records. Table 2.1 shows

Table 2.1. Loan Profitability Analysis

Profit Component	Unit Value
Average loan size	$15,500
Average loan yield	9.75%
Average cost of funds (including branch costs)	5.50%
Direct costs for consumer lending	0.82%
Corporate overhead	1.61%
Net profit per loan	1.82%

the components that went into the calculation of the net profit per loan.

The first step was to determine the yield from the loans, which was available from bank records. Next, the average difference between the cost of funds and the yield received on the loans was calculated. For example, the bank could obtain funds from depositors at 5.5 percent on average, including the cost of operating the branches. Next, the direct costs of making the loan, such as salaries of employees directly involved in consumer lending and advertising costs for consumer loans, had to be subtracted. Historically, such direct costs had amounted to 0.82 percent of the loan value. To cover overhead costs for other corporate functions, an additional 1.61 percent was subtracted. The remaining 1.82 percent of the average loan value represented the bank's profit margin on a loan. For example, if a loan is made in the amount of $1.5 million, the profit (value) of the loan to the bank would be $27,300 ($1.5 million × 1.82% profit margin = $27,300).

The advantage of this technique for calculating the value of increased output is that standard values are often available for many measures. The challenge is to quickly find appropriate and credible values for the desired measures. In the preceding bank example, the desired values had already been developed for other purposes and thus were available for use in the evaluation of the sales seminar program.

Case Example: Snapper Lawn Mowers

One of the more important measures of output is productivity, particularly for organizations in a highly competitive environment. Today, most organizations competing in the global economy do an excellent job of monitoring productivity and placing a value on it. Consider, for example, the Snapper lawn mower factory in McDonough, Georgia. Ten years ago, it produced 40 models of outdoor equipment items; now it makes 145. Ten years ago, all the manufacturing processes were performed by humans. Today robots do the welding, lasers cut parts, and computers control the steel-stamping process. Productivity at the factory is three times what it was ten years ago, and the workforce has been cut by half (Fishman, 2006). The value of this increased productivity can be calculated by the value of one new mower produced with the same resources. The value would be the portion of the revenue generated from the sale of the mower that is gross operating profit. At Snapper, each factory worker's output is measured every hour, every day, every month, and every year. And each person's performance is posted publicly every day for all to see. Production at the Snapper plant is rescheduled every week according to the pace of store sales across the nation. A computer juggles work assignments and balances the various parts of the assembly process. At Snapper, productivity is important; therefore, it is measured and valued. Snapper knows the value of improving productivity by an infinitesimal amount; the president knows that the factory must be aggressively efficient to compete in a global market with low-cost products. This requires that the performance of every factory worker be measured every hour of every day.

More Examples of Standard Values for Output Measures

In the Snapper case, monetary values for output have been developed. Snapper calculates the value of one unit of productivity; other organizations calculate the value of one item sold or some other output measure. For example, in a large retail store chain, a program was developed to increase sales at the store level. To determine the payoff, the evaluation team used the store-level profit margin of 2 percent, a measure that had been previously developed and that was listed in the company's annual report. When converting a sale to profit, this 2 percent margin was the multiplier that resulted in the monetary contribution to the store.

Using a profit margin instead of actual sales in an ROI calculation is an important issue. If this is done the true picture of the value added to the organization is not presented. A product sold or a service provided always incurs a cost, and the profit margin is a measure that subtracts out that cost. So the profit margin alone does not show the impact of the program; it needs to be applied to the actual sales data. Therefore, the true value added by a program, which must go into an ROI calculation, is the sales data multiplied by the profit margin.

In another example, the value of a new policyholder for an insurance company was calculated based on how long a customer could be expected to be with the insurance company and the money that would be made from a typical policy. Obviously, this value would vary with the product line—for example, automobile insurance versus homeowner's insurance versus life insurance. The insurance company has historical data on the length of time that policies have been held and the profit that has been made from the policies. This information is used to calculate the value of a new client (that is, the amount of money the company can expect to make, on average, when a new policy is written).

Table 2.2 provides additional detail on common measures of output data. As the table shows, standard values for output data are almost always available within an organization. However, if no value has been developed for a measure, one of the techniques discussed in this book can be used to develop the value.

Converting Quality to Monetary Value

Because quality is a critical issue, its cost is an important measure in most manufacturing and service firms. And because many programs are designed to improve quality, the program staff must place a value on improvement in relevant quality measures. For some quality measures, the task of assigning a monetary value is easy. For example, if quality is measured by means of a defect rate, the value of improvement is the cost of repairing or replacing a defective product. The most obvious cost of poor quality is the scrap or waste generated by mistakes. Defective products, spoiled raw materials, and discarded paperwork are all the results of poor quality.

Table 2.2. Common Output Measures and the Methods for Converting Output Data to a Monetary Value

Output Measure	Example	Method for Conversion to a Monetary Value	Comments
Unit of production	One unit assembled	Standard value	Value is available in almost every manufacturing unit.
Unit of service provided	One package delivered on time	Standard value	Value is developed in most service companies.
Sales	Monetary increase in revenue	Standard value (profit margin)	The profit from one additional dollar of sales is usually a standard value.
Market share	10 percent increase in market share in one year	Standard value	Margin on increased sales is usually a standard value.
Productivity	10 percent change in productivity index. For example an improvement in percentage of shipments per month.	Standard value	Such measures are specific to the type of production or productivity measured. Such measures may represent productivity per unit of time.

This scrap and waste translates directly to a monetary value. For example, in a production environment, the cost of a defective product is the total cost incurred to the point the mistake is identified minus the salvage value. In a service environment, the cost of a defective service is the cost incurred up to the point at which the deficiency is identified plus the cost to correct the problem, plus the cost to make the customer happy, plus the cost of the loss of customer loyalty.

Employee errors can cause expensive rework. The most costly rework occurs when a defective product is delivered to a customer and must be returned for correction. The cost of rework includes both labor and direct costs. In some organizations, the cost of rework can be as much as 35 percent of operating costs (Campanella, 1999).

Quality Cost Categories

Quality costs can be grouped into six major categories (Rust, Zahorik, and Keiningham, 1994):

1. *Internal failure* represents costs associated with problems detected prior to product shipment or service delivery. Typically, such costs are for rework and retesting.

2. *Penalty costs* are fines or penalties incurred as a result of unacceptable quality.

3. *External failure* refers to problems detected after product shipment or service delivery. Typical items in this category include technical support, complaint investigation, remedial upgrades, and fixes.

4. *Appraisal costs* are the expenses involved in determining the condition of a particular product or service. Typical appraisal costs involve testing and related activities, such as product quality audits.

5. *Prevention costs* involve efforts undertaken to avoid unacceptable products or service quality. These efforts include service quality management, inspections, process studies, and improvements.

6. *Customer dissatisfaction* is perhaps the costliest element of inadequate quality. In some cases, serious mistakes result in lost business. Customer dissatisfaction is difficult to quantify, and arriving at a monetary value through direct methods may be impossible. The judgment and expertise of sales, marketing, or quality managers are usually the best resources to draw on in measuring the impact of dissatisfaction. Increasingly, quality experts are measuring customer and client dissatisfaction through market surveys.

A tremendous number of quality measures have been converted to standard values. These measures include, but are not limited to, the following:

- Defects

- Rework

- Processing errors

- Accidents

- Grievances

- Equipment downtime

- System downtime

- Delay

- Fines

- Number of days sales uncollected

- Queues

Examples of Measures Converted to Quality Cost

In one example, a program focused on customer service provided by dispatchers in an oil company. The dispatchers processed orders and scheduled deliveries of fuel to service stations. A level of quality that was considered unsatisfactory was the number of pullouts experienced. A pullout occurs when a delivery truck cannot fill an order for fuel at a service station and the truck must return to the terminal for an adjustment to the order. In essence, this is a rework item. The average cost of a pullout was developed by tabulating the cost from a sampling of actual pullouts. The elements of the tabulation included driver time, the cost of the truck while adjusting the load, the cost of terminal use, and extra administrative expenses. The value that was developed became the accepted standard in the company. Organizations like this one have made great progress in developing standard values for the cost of quality.

In another example, a program was implemented for new couriers with DHL Worldwide Express in Spain. Several measures were used to evaluate the payoff of the program. One was a quality measure known as repackaging error. A repacking error occurs when a parcel is damaged due to mishandling and has to be repackaged before it can be delivered to the customer. The time and repackaging costs are small; nevertheless, when the repackaging errors across the country are tabulated, the value can be significant. It turned out that the quality office in Brussels had already developed a cost for this error, so that standard value was used in the ROI evaluation of the courier program.

This next example involves the cost of customer complaints. A large international firm, Global Financial Services, which offers a variety of financial services to its clients, embarked on a technological solution to improve management of customer contact. The software, called ACT!™, was designed to turn contacts into relationships and relationships into increased sales. The software was rolled out in a one-day workshop that taught participants how to use the software. The workshop consisted of three groups of thirty relationship managers, for a total of ninety. Among the impact measures driven by the program were customer complaints. The program was designed to reduce the number of customer complaints caused by excessive delays in responding or by miscommunications in those responses. Because this was a critical measure, the company had taken some steps to develop the value for a complaint. Also, because costs often increase over time, the value of a complaint needs to be adjusted each year, using the producer price index. At the time of this study, $4,610 was used as the cost of a complaint. In other words, if a complaint could be avoided, it would save the organization $4,610. This value included the time involved in resolving the complaint, the value of services and adjustments provided to the complaining party, and the potential loss of business as a result of the situation.

In many organizations, a great deal of effort has been put into developing and improving values for quality measures, due, in part, to total quality management, continuous process improvement, and Six Sigma. All these processes have focused on individual quality measures and the cost of quality. As a result, specific standard values have been developed.

Converting Employee Time to Monetary Value

A reduction in the use of employee time is a typical objective for an organizational program. In a team environment, a program might enable teams to perform tasks in a shorter time frame or with fewer people. On an individual basis, time management workshops are designed to help professional, sales, supervisory, and managerial employees save time in performing daily tasks. The value of time saved is often an important measure of a program's success; fortunately, converting data on time saved to a monetary value is a relatively easy process.

The most obvious value involved in employee time savings is reduction of the labor costs of performing the work. The monetary savings are found by multiplying the hours saved by the labor cost per hour. For example, after attending a time management program, participants estimated that they saved an average of seventy-four minutes per day, worth $31.25 per day or $7,500 per year. These values for the time savings were based on the participants' average salary plus benefits.

Using the average wage with a percentage added for employee benefits is appropriate for most calculations. However, employee time may be worth more. For example, additional costs in maintaining an employee (office space, furniture, telephone, utilities, computers, secretarial support, and other overhead expenses) could be included in the average labor cost. Therefore, the average wage rate could quickly escalate to a larger number. However, the conservative approach is to use the salary plus employee benefits.

In addition to reduced labor cost per hour, other benefits can result from a time savings. Such benefits include improved service, avoidance of penalties for late projects, and creation of additional opportunities for profit.

Case Example: A Technology Company

A case example will illustrate the conversion of time savings to a monetary value. A firm that produced telecommunication equipment was concerned about the excessive amount of time that engineers were spending in meetings. The initial assessment indicated that meetings might be longer than necessary, that some of the meetings could be avoided, and that too many individuals participated in meetings. Project-related meetings occupied a significant amount of time in the organization. A meeting management program was implemented to address all three concerns uncovered through the initial assessment: number of meetings, meeting duration, and number of meeting participants. The result was significant reductions in those three measures, which translated into time savings. The value used for the time savings was the average salary of the participants, estimated from human resources records by using the midpoint value of the job classifications of the meeting participants. The average salary was adjusted by the standard benefits factor to arrive at a cost of $31 per hour. To add credibility to the calculation, the evaluators took two additional steps. First, participants were asked what percentage of their time saved was actually spent on other productive work. Next, participants were asked to provide examples of other productive work. Addressing these two issues helped make the value more credible.

A Word of Caution

A word of caution is in order when a value for time savings is being developed. Benefits from time savings are realized only when the amount of time saved translates into an additional contribution. If a program results in a time savings for a specific manager, a monetary benefit will be realized only if the manager uses the additional time productively. If a team-based program generates a new process that eliminates several hours of work each day, actual savings will be realized only if costs decrease because of a reduction in employees, a reduction in overtime pay, or increased productivity. Therefore, an important preliminary step in developing a value for time savings is to determine whether a *true* savings will be realized.

True time savings can be arrived at in a variety of ways:

- A reduction of people employed, if the time savings involves a large number of individuals

- A reduction in hours worked, especially if the individuals involved are contract employees or are working overtime

- Finding out how much of the time savings is related directly to the program (isolating the effects of the program)

- Determining what percentage of the time savings has been used for other productive work

- Providing examples of the productive work facilitated by the time savings (such examples may also provide insight into how the time savings have been generated)

Such adjustments are critical in order to ensure that reporting of time savings is credible. Otherwise, key audience members may view the time savings as "funny money"; some chief financial officers indicate that if a benefit does not show up in the cost statements, then they will not count it. This is a hard-nosed approach that increases the importance of taking steps to ensure that time savings data are credible.

Why Standard Values Are Developed

Perhaps a recap of why standard values have been developed, particularly in recent years, will be helpful. Measures that matter are labeled as such because they are important to an organization, and therefore executives need to know their contribution or their value. Naturally, the impact of problems that lead to the implementation of programs is often defined in terms of these measures that matter and also needs to be converted to a monetary value. Most organizations have experienced a variety of process improvement programs—for example, transformation, reengineering, and reinvention. These programs provide structure and a process for driving improvements. Often, an important part of process improvement programs is not only fine tuning, revising, or amplifying the measurement process but also converting the measures to monetary values so that the magnitude of the process improvements can be shown.

Finally, activity-based costing has become important as the accounting field has placed more emphasis on calculating the monetary value of activities and processes. Often, a new measure, such as the cost of providing a service, is based on a series of activities that have already been valued in monetary terms. Thus research on these activities and their applications has resulted in more standard values for a variety of output items.

Standard Values Are Everywhere

As this chapter has illustrated, standard values have been developed for and are located in various parts of every organization. Exhibit 2.1 lists some of the many functions that have developed standard values. As we mentioned at the beginning of this chapter, in the ROI Methodology, a standard value is defined as an accepted monetary value placed on a unit of measure. The output measures so valued represent cost savings or profits. Output in the form of sales, new customers, market share, or customer loyalty adds value through additional profits obtained from additional sales. Output that is not connected to profits, such as the output of an individual work group, can be converted to cost savings. For example, if the output of a work group can be increased as a result of a program, with no additional resources required to drive the output, then the

Exhibit 2.1. Functions That Generate Standard Values

- Finance, accounting
- Production, manufacturing
- Operations, methods
- Engineering, technical support
- Information technology
- Marketing, customer service
- Procurement, logistics, supply chain
- Research and development
- Human resources

Figure 2.1. Converting Hard Data to Monetary Values

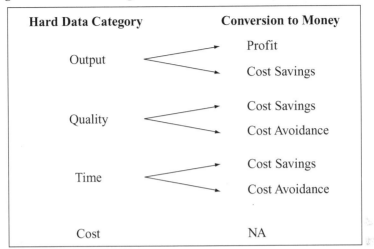

Hard Data Category	Conversion to Money
Output	Profit
	Cost Savings
Quality	Cost Savings
	Cost Avoidance
Time	Cost Savings
	Cost Avoidance
Cost	NA

corresponding value of the program is a cost savings (that is, additional output achieved for the same cost or decreased cost per unit of output). In the end, when converting data to money, the conversion is based on making money (profit), saving money, or avoiding costs. Figure 2.1 summarizes this process.

Perhaps no field has better developed standard values than sales and marketing. Table 2.3 shows examples of standard values from sales and marketing. As this table demonstrates, a tremendous number of standard values have been developed in sales and marketing, illustrating the strides in collecting standard values for output made in that field.

Final Thoughts

Standard values are everywhere. This chapter reinforces this statement by discussing several sources of standard values. The chapter also shows how standard values can be used as part of an ROI evaluation. They should come from credible sources, and when more than one standard value is located, the most credible—or if

Table 2.3. Examples of Standard Values from Sales and Marketing

Metric	Definition	Notes on Conversion to Monetary Value
Sales	Sale of the product or service, recorded in a variety of ways—for example, by product, by time period, by customer	The data must be converted to a monetary value by applying the profit margin for a particular sales category.
Profit margin (percentage)	$\dfrac{\text{Price} - \text{Cost}}{\text{Cost}}$ for the product, customer, or time period	Factor for converting sales to monetary value added to the organization.
Unit margin	Unit price less unit cost	This measure shows the value of incremental sales.
Channel margin	Channel profits as a percentage of the product's selling price in that channel	This measure shows the value of sales through a particular marketing channel.
Retention rate	Ratio of customers retained to the number of customers at risk of leaving	The value of this measure is the money saved by not having to acquire a replacement customer.
Churn rate	Ratio of customers who leave to the number who are at risk of leaving	The value of this measure is the money saved by not having to acquire a replacement customer.
Customer profit	Difference between the revenues earned from and the cost associated with a customer relationship during the specified period	The monetary value added is the profit obtained from customers. It all goes toward the bottom line.
Customer value, lifetime	Present value of the future cash flows attributed to a customer relationship	This is a bottom-line measure; as customer value increases, it adds directly to profits. Also, when a customer is added, the incremental value is the customer lifetime value average.

Cannibalization rate	Percentage of new product sales taken from existing product lines	This measure should be minimized because it represents an adverse effect on existing products; the value added is the loss of profits due to the loss of sales in the existing product lines.
Workload	Hours required to service clients and prospects	The cost of this measure includes the salaries, commissions, and benefits paid for workload hours.
Inventories	Total amount of product or brand available for sale in a particular channel	Because inventories are valued at the cost of carrying the inventory, costs involve space, handling, and the time value of money. Insufficient inventory results in the cost of expediting the new inventory or the loss of sales because of the inventory outage.
Market share	Sales revenue as a percentage of total market sales	Actual sales are converted to monetary values through the profit margins. This is a measure of competitiveness.
Loyalty	The length of time the customer stays with the organization, the willingness to pay a premium, and the willingness to search for a brand or product	The value of this measure is calculated as the profit from the sale or the additional profit on the premium.

Source: Adapted from Farris, Bendle, Pfeifer, and Ribstein, 2006, pp. 46–47.

all are credible, the lowest—should be used. When standard values are not available, other methods must be used to find the monetary value of the measures that matter. The next chapter discusses one such method: calculating the value.

References

Campanella, J. (ed.). *Principles of Quality Costs.* (3rd ed.) Milwaukee, Wis.: American Society for Quality, 1999.

Farris, P. W., Bendle, N. T., Pfeifer, P. E., and Ribstein, D. J. *Marketing Metrics: 50+ Metrics Every Executive Should Master.* Upper Saddle River, N.J.: Wharton School Publishing, 2006.

Fishman, C. *The Wal-Mart Effect: How the World's Most Powerful Company Really Works—and How It's Transforming the American Economy.* New York: Penguin Books, 2006.

Rust, R., Zahorik, A., and Keiningham, R. *Return on Quality: Measuring the Financial Impact of Your Company's Quest for Quality.* Chicago: Probus, 1994.

3

Calculate the Value

I f a standard value is not available for a desired measure, one logical approach is to calculate its monetary value. This chapter discusses two basic approaches. One is to use cost statements, reports, or records to develop the value. This approach can be time-consuming and is not always recommended because of the excessive resources that may be required. The second approach is to try to develop links between the measure in question, one that is difficult to convert to a monetary value, and some other measure that can be converted more easily. The upside is that much progress has been made in showing links between hard-to-measure data and other, easy-to-measure data. The downside is that finding these connections is difficult. We suggest that evaluators should not try to calculate a relationship but should try to find one that has already been developed.

Using Historical Costs

Sometimes, historical records contain the value of a measure or reveal the cost (or value) of a unit of improvement. This technique involves identifying the appropriate records and tabulating the cost components of the measure in question. For example, a large construction firm implemented a program to improve safety performance. The program improved several safety-related performance measures, ranging from OSHA fines to total workers' compensation costs. Using one year of data from the company's records, the staff calculated the average value of improvements in each safety measure.

Key Issues in Using Records and Reports

The technique of developing monetary values from historical records, while credible, can be difficult to use for several reasons. The first and perhaps the most important issue is the amount of time required to calculate the values. This technique often involves securing a variety of records and calculating an average. For example, a financial services firm in Tel Aviv was interested in demonstrating the value of an ethics program. One of the payoff measures was a reduction in expense account violations, whether intentional or unintentional. Calculating the cost of an expense account violation required that an evaluator add up the last fifty violations. It took a lot of effort to pore over the records, determine the money lost due to each violation, add the numbers, and determine the average value. Again, using historical records is a credible method, but it often requires too much time.

Another issue is availability of data. Sometimes, all the data are not available and exhaustive searching may be necessary to find exactly what is needed. Still another issue is access to the data. In some situations, the individual conducting the evaluation may not have access to the data. Some of the data may be considered off-limits or proprietary and thus may not be available for use in the evaluation. Accuracy of the data is yet another consideration. Records, although they appear precise, may not be accurate.

Inaccuracy leads to a final concern: estimation. While records may clearly indicate direct expenses, this information often represents only part of the cost. Other costs may have to be estimated. For example, the cost of employee turnover may include costs that are not indicated in the records. While the direct costs of replacing an individual—for instance, the costs of recruiting, selection, orientation, and initial training—are easily available from the records, other costs—such as those associated with disruption, bottlenecks, lost productivity, or lost knowledge—are not readily available from the records, if at all. Therefore, even though historical records are being used to develop a monetary value, estimates would have to be used in the calculation.

For all of these reasons, historical records are usually used to convert data to a monetary value only when the sponsor, the key client, wants to know the cost of the item because it has not been previously developed.

A word of caution is in order. If the historical records approach is used to convert data to monetary value, this part of the evaluation may require more time, effort, or money than has been budgeted for the entire ROI evaluation. The client should be made aware of this possibility, and it might be desirable to assign responsibility for developing the value of the data to other, more suitable parties.

All of the issues in this section need to be addressed during the evaluation planning stage discussed in *ROI Fundamentals*, the first book in this series.

Case Study: A Metropolitan Transit Authority

Here is a detailed example of the historical records approach.

A large city had implemented an absenteeism reduction program for its bus drivers. The vice president of human resources was interested in presenting the return on investment for the program. To show the impact of the program, a value for the cost of one absence was needed. As part of the study, an external consulting firm developed a detailed cost of one absence, including the full costs of a driver pool that included 231 substitute drivers, in order to cover unexpected absences.

While several approaches could have been taken in order to determine the cost of absenteeism, the analysis at Metro Transit Authority was based on the cost of replacement driver staffing. Substitute drivers, as well as the regular drivers, were expected to work an average of 240 days per year, leaving 20 days for vacation, holidays, and sick days. The average wage for a substitute driver was $33,500 per year, and the employee benefits factor was 38 percent of payroll. When a regular driver was unexpectedly absent, he or she could charge the absence to either sick leave or vacation, substituting a planned paid day (vacation) for the unexpected absence. This was almost always what occurred. Because of this system, the cost of absenteeism was minimized. When there was a perfect match between the number of absences and the number of substitute drivers, the cost of the driver pool was for vacation coverage.

However, substitute driver staffing was not always at the exact level needed for a specific day's unscheduled absences. The planned number of substitute drivers was a function of expected absenteeism. Because of the service problems that could develop as a result of understaffing, for most days overstaffing of substitute drivers was planned. To minimize potential delays, all substitute drivers were required to report to work each day. Substitute drivers not used in driver seats essentially performed no productive work that could be counted as added value. During the previous year, overstaffing had occurred on about 75 percent of the weekdays and nonholidays. This overstaffing represented 4,230 days of wasted time. On weekends and holidays, overstaffing had occurred almost half the time, representing a total of 570 wasted days.

On some days, a shortage of substitute drivers occurred, which caused the buses to run late; in those cases, overtime was used to make the adjustment. During the last year, there had been sixty-five instances in which a driver was not available, and it was estimated that in forty-five of those situations, a regular driver was paid double time to fill in the schedule.

A final and significant cost of absenteeism, beyond the salaries and benefits of the substitute drivers, was the cost of recruiting, training, maintaining, and supervising the substitute driver pool. This item included recruiting and employment, training and preparation, office space, administration and coordination, and

Exhibit 3.1. The Cost of Absenteeism at Metro Transit Authority

Average daily cost of wages and benefits for a substitute driver:

$$\$33,500 \times 1.38 \div 240 = \$192.63$$

Cost of overstaffing, weekdays:

$$\$192.63 \times 4,230 = \$814,800$$

Cost of overstaffing, weekends and holidays:

$$\$192.63 \times 570 = \$109,800$$

Cost of understaffing, overtime:

$$\$192.63 \times 45 = \$8,670$$

Cost of recruiting, training, maintaining, and supervising the driver pool:

$$\$33,500 \times 231 \times 0.25 = \$1,934,600$$

Total cost of absenteeism = $2,867,070

supervision. This item was estimated to be equal to 25 percent of the substitute drivers' annual pay. Exhibit 3.1 illustrates how the total direct cost of absenteeism was developed from the preceding information.

As this impact study revealed, developing historical costs can sometimes be expensive and time-consuming, leading evaluators to look for an easier way. Using historical cost data may not be the technique of choice because of the time, effort, and costs involved. In those situations, one or more of the other techniques discussed in this book should be used.

Linking with Other Measures

When standard values and historical records are unavailable or inappropriate, a feasible approach might be to find a relationship between the measure in question and some other measure that can

Exhibit 3.2. Classic Relationships

Job satisfaction	connected to	Turnover
Job satisfaction	connected to	Absenteeism
Job satisfaction	connected to	Customer satisfaction
Organizational commitment	connected to	Productivity
Engagement	connected to	Productivity
Customer satisfaction	connected to	Revenue
Conflicts	connected to	Productivity

be easily converted to a monetary value. This approach involves identifying relationships in which there is a strong correlation between one measure and another with a standard value.

Classic Relationships

Fortunately, in the last two decades, many relationships between measures within organizations have been found. Exhibit 3.2 lists some of these classic relationships. Success in using the linking technique comes from finding these relationships that have already been worked out. These relationships have been figured out because the organization has an interest in understanding the connections between the measures.

For example, consider the classic relationship shown in Figure 3.1: the relationship between customer satisfaction and revenue from those customers. This is perhaps the relationship that is most commonly examined because it seems logical to conclude that customer satisfaction and revenue are related. Customers are more satisfied, so they purchase more products or they continue to be a customer. In most organizations, this relationship exists, and today a majority of larger organizations have examined this connection.

Figure 3.1. A Classic Relationship Between Customer Satisfaction and Revenue

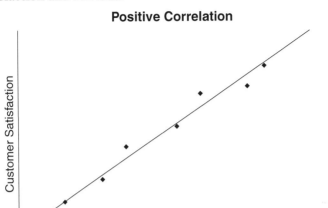

The important point is that when a program results in increased customer satisfaction, then revenue increases, giving the organization a direct payoff. Both customer satisfaction and revenue may be program objectives, and both may be payoff measures that are driven by the program. In that situation, customer satisfaction would be listed as an intangible measure, because the method of converting customer satisfaction to a monetary value (making it tangible) uses the connection of customer satisfaction to revenue, which is already included in the evaluation as a payoff measure. It is important not to count this value twice. However, if revenue is not used as a measure in the evaluation but is used only to show the monetary value of the improved customer satisfaction, the established relationship between the two measures provides an opportunity to show that payoff.

Case Example: A European Postal Service

The relationship illustrated in Figure 3.2 represents a correlation between job satisfaction and employee turnover. In a postal

Figure 3.2. The Relationship Between Job Satisfaction and Turnover

service program designed to improve job satisfaction, a monetary value needed to be assigned to changes in the job satisfaction index. A predetermined relationship showing a correlation between improvements in job satisfaction and reductions in turnover for specific groups linked the changes in job satisfaction directly to turnover. These data sets were taken from the human capital system. Through the use of a standard value, the cost of turnover can easily be calculated. As a result, a change in job satisfaction is converted to an approximate monetary value. Such a valuation is not always exact because of error and other factors, but this type of estimate may be sufficient for converting job satisfaction to a monetary value.

Case Example: Sears, Roebuck and Company

In some situations, a chain of relationships may be established to show the connection between two or more variables. In this approach, a measure that may be difficult to convert to a monetary

Figure 3.3. Link Between Job Satisfaction and Revenue at Sears, Roebuck and Company

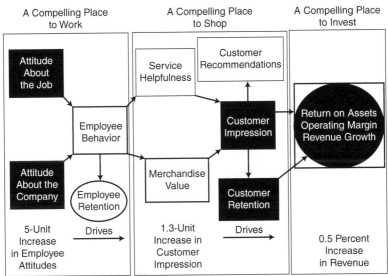

Source: Rucci, Kirn, and Quinn, 1998, p. 83. Used with permission. Copyright 1998 by the President and Fellows of Harvard College.

value is linked to other measures that, in turn, are linked to measures on which a value can be placed. Ultimately, the measures are linked to a monetary value that is often based on profits. Figure 3.3 shows the model used by Sears, one of the world's largest retail chains (Rucci, Kirn, and Quinn, 1998). The model connects job attitudes (collected directly from the employees) with customer service, which is directly related to revenue growth. The shaded measures are collected and distributed in the form of Sears total performance indicators. The rectangles in the chart represent survey information, while the ovals represent hard data.

As the model shows, a 5-point improvement in employee attitudes will drive a 1.3-point improvement in customer satisfaction. This, in turn, drives a 0.5 percent increase in revenue growth.

Therefore, if employee attitudes at a local store improved by 5 points and previous revenue growth was 5 percent, the new revenue growth would be 5.5 percent.

Links between measures such as those just described, often called the *service-profit chain*, create a promising way to place monetary values on measures that are difficult to quantify.

Concerns When Using Relationships Between Measures to Assign Monetary Values

This section presents some pros and cons about the use of relationships between measures to assign monetary values. One advantage is that many of these relationships have been figured out, though not necessarily as part of an ROI study. However, if a relevant relationship has not been worked out, attempting to figure out one of these relationships simply to convert one data item to a monetary value would likely allocate too much time and too many resources to that one issue. One must keep the issue in perspective, remembering that the item is only one measure in one part of the ROI evaluation. To exhaust days or weeks of time and resources in an attempt to convert one data item to a monetary value would be unadvisable. For this reason, the recommended approach is to find a relationship between measures that has already been established.

However, if no relevant relationship has been worked out, that fact may bring up an important issue. When attempting to convert soft data—a typical category of hard-to-value data—to a monetary value, it may be helpful to raise the issue that there has been no work within the organization to convert it to money; that is, classical relationships have not been developed. Calling attention to this need may lead to another project, but that project will be beyond the scope of the team conducting the ROI evaluation. As discussed earlier, the cost in time and money of such a study would likely exceed the value of the evaluation itself.

Final Thoughts

This chapter has presented two credible approaches for converting data to monetary values. The first, calculating the cost of a data item by using records, cost statements, and reports, often involves adding up the costs of repeated incidents and averaging them to get the cost of one unit. The second technique involves finding a link between the hard-to-value measure and an easy-to-value measure. While both of these are credible methods, they may require too much time and effort if the data are not readily available or the relevant relationships have not already been determined. These techniques are useful, but they must be used with caution. When the techniques described in this chapter are not feasible, then the next source of data is research—conducted either by speaking with experts or by perusing the databases. These techniques are described in the next chapter.

Reference

Rucci, A., Kirn, S., and Quinn, R. "The Employee-Customer-Profit Chain at Sears." *Harvard Business Review*, Jan./Feb. 1998, 76(1), 82–98.

4

Find the Value

This chapter presents two easy and credible techniques for converting data to monetary values. The first is to have experts from within or outside an organization place a monetary value on a unit of measure, using their knowledge and experience. The second technique is to search databases in order to find a value for the unit of measure in question. Many databases are accessible on the Internet, making this an easy-to-use method that generates abundant information.

Using Internal and External Experts

When faced with converting soft data items to monetary values when historical records or standard values are often not available, obtaining input from experts may be an appropriate solution. In this approach, experts provide the value of one unit of measure. Individuals who have knowledge of the situation under evaluation as well as the respect of the management group are often the best choices to provide expert input. These experts must understand the processes and must be willing to provide values as well as the assumptions used in arriving at the values. When requesting input from experts, it is best to explain the full scope of what is needed, providing as many specifics as possible. Most experts will have their own method of determining a value.

Working with Internal Experts

Internal experts are relatively easy to find. Many times, the expert is located in the obvious department or has an obvious job title. For example, in a BlueCross BlueShield affiliate, a program was being implemented to lower the number of customer appeals. An appeal occurs when a customer requests that an insurance company reconsider its decision in regard to the payment or coverage of an item. To calculate the ROI, the cost of one appeal was needed. A standard value had not been developed for this measure, so a logical choice was to go to the customer appeals department (the obvious department), which had several customer appeals coordinators (the obvious job title). These individuals were knowledgeable about the issues involved when an insurance claim was appealed and dealt with these issues daily. They were credible and were in the best position to offer a credible value for the measure.

Another way to find an expert is to trace the origin of a report. Many data items come from a report generated by a department or a function. The individual who sends the report may know the value of the measure or may know the person who would be in the best position to provide relevant data. If the identity of the individual who generated the report is unknown or unclear, the organization directory might indicate who within the organization could address the issue. If all else fails, ask someone. Asking others can narrow the search to the individual or individuals who know the information best.

Several issues must be addressed when asking an internal expert to provide a monetary value. First is the expert's experience. The most experienced individuals should provide the value. Another issue is conflicts of interest. Do the experts have a reason for wanting the value of the measure to be large or small? Sometimes, a bias is present. For example, in the BlueCross BlueShield case, if the customer appeals coordinators providing the information had felt that their workload was too heavy and that they did not have time to handle the appeals, they might have placed a higher value on the number of appeals processed in order to bring the matter to the attention of the management team. It is important that the experts who provide the monetary value be neutral.

Working with External Experts

When internal experts are not available, external experts are often sought. Like internal experts, external experts must be selected on the basis of their experience with the unit of measure. Fortunately, many experts are available who work directly with important measures such as creativity, innovation, employee attitudes, customer satisfaction, employee turnover, absenteeism, and grievances. They are often willing to provide values for these items. Consider the credibility and reputation of the expert carefully; these factors are critical, because the credibility of the value will be directly related to the expert's reputation.

The credibility of external experts is often determined by their credentials. Sometimes, the expert's credentials involve certifications, degrees, or experience in a relevant area. Credibility could also be based on an individual's publications; writing articles, studies, or books about the subject in question can add to an expert's credibility. Consulting experience can also qualify an individual as an expert. Finally, a track record in offering a value for a measurement and having that value verified through other analysis is another positive credential. Above all, the individual must be neutral in regard to the value, with no bias toward assigning either a high or a low value.

Case Example: A Manufacturing Plant

An example will help clarify the process of consulting an internal expert. In one manufacturing plant, a team-building program was designed to reduce the number of grievances that proceeded to step 2 in the plant's four-step grievance resolution process. Step 2 was when the grievance was recorded in writing and became a measurable data item. Except for the costs of settlements and direct external costs, the company had no records on the total costs of grievances. (For example, there were no data on the time required to resolve a grievance.) Therefore, a value from an expert was needed. The manager of labor relations, who had credibility with senior management and thorough knowledge of the grievance process, provided an estimate of the cost. He based his estimate on the average settlement when a grievance was lost; direct costs related to grievances (arbitration, legal fees, printing, research); the estimated amount of supervisory, staff, and employee time associated with grievances; and a factor for reduced morale and other "soft" consequences. This internally generated, estimated value, while not a precise figure, was appropriate for this analysis and had adequate credibility with management.

Case Example: A Health Care Firm

Sometimes, two or more methods may be used in combination to develop monetary values. In a study involving a health care firm, the cost of a formal complaint filed with the vice president of human resources was evaluated. In this analysis, it was assumed that if no complaints were filed, there would be no costs of communication, investigation, or defense associated with sexual harassment. Two approaches were used to arrive at the cost of a complaint. First, the direct cost of all activities and processes connected with sexual harassment for an entire year was captured. This figure was taken directly from cost statements. Second, the other costs (for example, staff and management time spent on these activities) were estimated, using input from internal experts—the EEOC and affirmative action staff. Figure 4.1 shows how these two values were combined to arrive at a total value of $852,000 for

Figure 4.1. Converting Data to Monetary Values by Combining Historical Costs and Expert Input

thirty-five complaints, or an approximate value of $24,000 for one complaint.

Using External Databases

For some soft data items, it may be appropriate to assign monetary values that are taken from the research of others. This strategy taps external databases containing studies and research projects that focus on the cost of data items. Fortunately, many databases contain cost studies on a variety of data items related to programs. Information is available on the cost of turnover, absenteeism, grievances, accidents, and even customer satisfaction. The difficulty lies in finding a database with studies or research on a situation similar to the program that is being evaluated. Ideally, the information would come from a similar setting in the same industry, but that is not always possible. Sometimes, information that relates to all industries or organizations can be sufficient, perhaps with an adjustment to fit the industry under consideration.

Internet Searches

For some, the Web holds the most promise for finding monetary values that are not readily available from standard values, historical records, or experts. Progress continues to be made in the use of Web searches to develop monetary values. A few guidelines for using the Web are presented later in this section.

General Web directories and portals may be very helpful. Although they have a bit in common with Web search engines, general Web directories such as Yahoo, Open Directory, and Look Smart also differ greatly. Although their databases may include less than 1 percent of what search engines cover, general Web directories can still help an evaluator locate needed information and in many cases may be the best starting point (Hock, 2004).

A specialized directory is more appropriate than the general Web directories for accessing Web resources on a specific topic. Such sites bring together well-organized collections of Internet resources on specific topics and provide an important starting point for research on monetary values of measures.

Search engines provide more possibilities for searches because of their vast coverage. General Web search engines such as AltaVista, AllTheWeb, and Google stand in contrast to a Web directory in three primary ways:

1. They are much larger, containing over a billion instead of a few million records.

2. Virtually no human selectivity is involved in determining which Web pages are included in the search engine's database.

3. They are designed for searching (responding to a user's specific query) rather than browsing and, therefore, provide much more substantial searching capabilities than directories.

Groups, mailing lists, and other interactive forums form a class of Internet resources that too few researchers take advantage of. They can be useful for a broad range of applications, including finding the monetary value of data. Because they can tap knowledge held only in people's minds, these tools can be gold mines of information not found elsewhere.

A range of news resources are also available online, including news services, newswires, newspapers, news consolidation services, and more. Because some studies centering on particular values are newsworthy, online news items can be excellent sources for those who are seeking to capture the value of specific types of data.

In general, Web searches are an important tool for the evaluator when it comes to collecting information on monetary values.

A typical concern about Web searches is the quality of the content. Some think that the Internet has low-quality content, although in reality, it is no different from other sources; for example, right alongside the high-quality publications available on newsstands are those with low-quality content. Nonetheless, here are a few guidelines to help evaluators obtain high-quality information from Web searches:

- *Consider the source.* From what organization does the content originate? Check to see that the organization is identified both on the Web page and in the URL. The URL will identify the owner, and the owner may be revealing in regard to the quality. Is the content identified as coming from known sources, such as a news organization, the government, an academic journal, a professional association, or a major investment firm?

- *Consider the motivation.* What is the purpose of this site—dissemination of academic research, consumer protection, sales, entertainment, or political dialogue? Considering the motivation behind a posting can be helpful in assessing the degree of objectivity.

- *Look at the quality of the writing.* If the content contains spelling and grammatical errors, the data may have quality problems as well.

• *Look at the quality of the source documentation.* First, remember that the number of footnotes is not necessarily an accurate measure of the quality of a work. On the other hand, if facts are cited, does the page identify the origin of the facts? Check out some of the cited sources to see whether the facts actually appear there.

• *Check whether the site and its content are as current as they should be.* If the site is reporting on current events, the need for currency and the answer to the question of currency will be apparent.

• *Use multiple sources to verify the facts used in the data conversion, or choose the most authoritative source.* Unfortunately, many facts given on Web pages are simply wrong, due to carelessness, exaggeration, guessing, or other factors. Often, they are wrong because the person creating the page content did not check the facts.

The preceding list provides some helpful ways to focus on the quality of information, which is crucial in a search for a credible monetary value for a particular measure.

Critical thinking should be applied to the information found and the claims that are made. Exhibit 4.1 provides some critical thinking questions to help the serious searcher find the right information (Berkman, 2004).

Case Example: A Regional Bank

An example will illustrate the use of databases to find a monetary value for a measure. A new program was designed to reduce turnover of branch employees in a regional banking group. To complete the evaluation and calculate the ROI, the cost of turnover was needed. To develop the turnover value internally, several costs would have to be identified, including the costs of recruiting, employment processing, orientation, training new employees, lost productivity while a new employee was being trained, quality problems, scheduling difficulties, and customer satisfaction problems. Additional costs included regional manager time spent on turnover issues and, in some cases, exit costs of litigation, severance, and unemployment. Obviously, these costs were significant. However, most

Exhibit 4.1. Ask the Right Questions When Searching the Web

Before going to the Web for business research, ask yourself:

- Why am I choosing the Web to perform this research?

  If it's because the Web is fast, why is that good?

  If it's because it's free, why is free information best? How much would I pay for good information?

- Is a search engine the best tool to find what I'm looking for on the Web?

- Where else might I find the same type of information?

- Would a library or a fee-based database contain the information I'm looking for?

When you find a source of interest on the Web, ask yourself:

- Who put this information on the Web? Why?

- If it's free, why did the creator make it that way?

- Who gains from having this information on the Web?

When evaluating the authority of the publisher or creator of the information, ask yourself:

- What are the qualifications of this person or organization?

- Why should I trust this person or organization?

- Why are these opinions being offered here?

If a search engine doesn't return the information you're looking for, ask yourself:

- Did I use all the appropriate keywords and phrases?

- Did I follow the search engine's instructions?

Exhibit 4.1. Ask the Right Questions When Searching the Web (Continued)

- Could the search engine have failed to index the site that includes the information?

- Could the information be online, but as part of the "invisible Web" that's inaccessible to search engines?

- Could it mean that the information isn't on the Web? If so, might it be available from other sources (for example, the library, a journal database, a book or directory, an association, an expert)?

- Could it be that what I'm looking for isn't the kind of information that's easily found on the Web? If so, am I better off trying a different type of resource altogether?

- Could it mean that the information simply doesn't exist?

When you find statistical data, ask yourself:

- What (or who or where) is the original source or creator of the data?

- Is this the most recent version or series of the data?

- Do I know the larger context from which these data were derived?

- Where can I find the methodologies and assumptions used to create these statistics?

On an online news site, ask yourself:

- What makes this a legitimate news-gathering and reporting site?

- What is a legitimate news-gathering and reporting site?

- Can I distinguish editorial content from advertising on this site?

Source: Adapted from Berkman, 2004.

program managers do not have the time to calculate the cost of turnover, particularly when it is needed only for a one-time event such as evaluating a program. In this case, turnover cost studies in the same industry placed the value at about 1.1 to 1.25 times the average annual salary of the employees. Most turnover cost studies report the cost of turnover as a multiple of annual base salaries. In this case, management decided to be conservative and adjusted the value down to 0.9 times the average annual base salary of the employees.

Case Example: A Federal Agency

In another example, a federal government agency wanted to reduce turnover among its communication specialists. The agency was experiencing turnover in the range of 35–40 percent in these highly specialized jobs. Over 1,500 individuals were in the job group, so the results of this turnover were disastrous. Unable to increase pay, the agency decided on a unique approach to the turnover problem, offering a master's degree program for communication specialists, to be attended on agency time. This program took three years to complete and was offered to specialists who had at least one year of service. The individuals involved in the program had to agree to two years of service after they received their master's degree. (For more details on this case study, see Phillips and Phillips, 2007.)

Although the monetary value of the program derived primarily from turnover reduction, value was also received from the graduate projects that were required for the specialists' degrees. To calculate the cost of turnover, an Internet search was conducted through ERIC. The search, available through EBSCO*host*, yielded a variety of studies that, when arranged by job group, yielded the information found in Table 4.1. The target group closely fit the specialist category, a fact that suggested that the cost of turnover was two to four times the annual salary. This number was higher than the human resources staff anticipated. As a compromise, a value of 1.75 times the annual salary was used. While this value was probably lower than the actual fully loaded cost of turnover, it was conservative to assign this value. It is much better to use a conservative value than to calculate the fully loaded costs, which would involve all the categories shown in note 2 of Table 4.1.

Table 4.1. Summary of Turnover Costs from an External Database

Job Type or Category	Turnover Costs as a Percentage of Annual Wages or Salary
Entry-level workers—hourly, nonskilled (for example, fast-food worker)	30–50%
Service and production workers—hourly (for example, courier)	40–70%
Skilled workers—hourly (for example, machinist)	75–100%
Clerical and administrative (for example, scheduler)	50–80%
Professional (for example, sales representative, nurse, accountant)	75–125%
Technical (for example, computer technician)	100–150%
Engineers (for example, chemical engineer)	200–300%
Specialists (for example, computer software designer)	200–400%
Supervisors and team leaders (for example, section supervisor)	100–150%
Middle managers (for example, department manager)	125–200%

General notes:

1. Percentages are rounded, to reflect the general range of costs from the studies.

Table 4.1. Summary of Turnover Costs from an External Database (*Continued*)

2. Costs are fully loaded to include all the costs of replacing an employee and bringing him or her to the level of productivity and efficiency of the former employee. The turnover included in the studies is usually unexpected and unwanted. The following cost categories are usually included:

- Exit cost of previous employee
- Recruiting cost
- Employee cost
- Orientation cost
- Training cost
- Wages and salaries while training
- Lost productivity

- Quality problems
- Customer dissatisfaction
- Loss of expertise and knowledge
- Supervisor's time on turnover issues
- Temporary replacement costs

3. Turnover costs are usually calculated when excessive turnover is an issue and turnover costs are high. The actual cost of turnover for a specific job in an organization may vary considerably. The ranges listed in this table are intended to reflect what has been generally reported in the literature when turnover costs are analyzed.

4. The sources of the data in this table fall into three general categories:

   (a) Industry and trade magazines that have reported the cost of turnover for a specific job within an industry.

   (b) Publications in general management (for both academics and practitioners), human resources management, human resources development, training, and performance improvement that publish ROI cost studies because of the importance of turnover to senior managers and human resources managers.

   (c) Independent studies that have been conducted by organizations and not reported in the literature. Some of these studies have been provided privately to the ROI Institute. In addition, the ROI Institute has conducted several turnover cost studies; these results are included in the table.

This brief example shows the potential value of using the Internet. Table 4.1 could serve as a useful guide to monetary values for other turnover studies. Other information similar to that in Table 4.1 can be easily obtained online.

Exhibit 4.2. Finding Data: A Variety of Databases

• Search engines	• Government databases
• Research databases	• Commercial databases
• Academic databases	• Association databases
• Industry and trade databases	• Professional databases

Other Sources of Databases

A variety of databases are available, and they are not found only on the Internet. Exhibit 4.2 lists some types of databases that are available. Industries, trade associations, government organizations, commercial organizations, and professional associations all represent excellent potential sources of databases. Often, these databases can be downloaded from the organization. Sometimes, they are only available on hard copy and obtaining them may involve a charge. Regardless of the source, the key is to find the most credible data available for the measures in question.

Final Thoughts

This chapter presents two techniques that hold promise for capturing the monetary value of a measure. Input from internal or external experts is usually easy to obtain and is often credible. Obtaining a value from an expert may take no more time than an e-mail or a phone call. The challenge in using this method is to ensure that the expert is the most credible source of information (Guiding Principle 3). Sometimes, external databases of data from previously developed studies are available. Using the Internet is an excellent way to find and use these databases. If the needed data are not found in Internet databases, other databases may provide the information needed to convert a measure to a monetary value. Using experts and drawing on information from external databases are credible techniques for finding the monetary value of a measure and are feasible for most programs. When experts and databases are unavailable, the next technique to consider is estimations. Their use in converting data to money is described next.

References

Berkman, R. *The Skeptical Business Searcher: The Information Advisor's Guide to Evaluating Web Data, Sites, and Sources.* Medford, N.J.: Information Today, 2004.

Hock, R. *The Extreme Searcher's Internet Handbook.* Medford, N.J.: CyberAge Books, 2004.

Phillips, P. P., and Phillips, J. J. *Proving the Value of HR: ROI Case Studies.* Birmingham, Ala.: ROI Institute, 2007.

5

Estimate the Value

This final chapter on the techniques for converting data to monetary values shows how to use estimates from a variety of sources. Using estimates is the technique of last resort for converting data to monetary values because of the perceived inaccuracy of estimates. The challenge when using estimates is to ensure that the data are taken from the most credible source, that they are adjusted for the error of the estimate, and that they are reported cautiously.

Using Estimates from Participants

In some situations, program participants are in the best position to estimate the value of improvement in soft data. This method is appropriate when participants are capable of providing estimates of the value of the unit of measure that was improved by implementation of the program. Participants should be provided with clear instructions, along with examples of the type of information needed. The advantage of this method is that the individuals closest to the improvement are often able to provide the most reliable estimates of its value.

Case Example: A Manufacturing Plant

An example will illustrate the process of having participants estimate the monetary value of a measure. A group of supervisors in a manufacturing plant attended an interpersonal skills program,

"Improving Work Habits," which was designed to lower the rate of absenteeism of employees in their work units. It was hoped that successful application of the program would result in a reduction in absenteeism. To calculate the ROI for the program, it was necessary to determine the average cost of one absence. As in most organizations, historical records on the cost of absenteeism were not available. Experts were not available, and external databases for that particular industry were sparse. As a result, supervisors (the program participants) were asked to estimate the cost of an absence.

In a group interview, each participant was asked to recall the last time an employee in his or her work group was unexpectedly absent and to describe what had to be done to compensate for the absence. Because the impact of an absence varies considerably from one employee to another even within the same work unit, the group listened to all explanations. After reflecting on what had to be done when an employee was absent, each supervisor was asked to provide an estimate of the average cost of an absence within the company. As is sometimes the case, some of the supervisors were reluctant to provide estimates, but with prodding and encouragement, they provided a value. They were also asked to state how confident they were in their estimates.

Each value given was adjusted by the confidence percentage of the person who provided the estimate. The adjusted values for the group were averaged, and the result was the estimated cost of an absence for use in the program evaluation. Although it was an estimate, this value was probably more accurate than data from external databases, calculations using internal records, or estimates from experts would have been. Because it came from supervisors who dealt with the issue daily, it was likely to have credibility with senior management.

Key Issues in Using Participant Estimates

One of the fundamental issues in using participants to estimate the monetary value of a measure is the credibility of those providing the estimate. In some cases, participants are in a position to provide the data, as the preceding example illustrates. However, in many cases, they are not. They may not know the full scope of the measure. This issue is different from the issue that occurs when participants isolate the effects of a program, which is discussed in *Isolation of Results*, book three in this series. In that situation, participants are often the most credible source because their performance has caused the change, and they can isolate the effects of the program based on their own changes in performance. However, when the task is placing a monetary value on a data item, the individual driving the performance may not appreciate all the consequences or all the impacts of the measure, all of which affect the monetary value.

Another issue is adjusting for the error of the estimate, as explained in the previous example. Asking the question "What is your confidence in the value that you have provided, on a scale of 0 percent (no confidence) to 100 percent (complete confidence)?" provides an adjustment factor that can be multiplied by the estimated value. Essentially, the confidence percentage is an error discount factor.

Using Estimates from Supervisors and Managers

In some situations, participants may be incapable of placing an accurate value on the improvement resulting from a program. Their work may be so far removed from the output of the process that they cannot reliably provide estimates. In these cases, their team leader, supervisor, or manager may be capable of providing estimates and may therefore be asked to provide a monetary value for a unit of improvement linked to the program. For example, a program for customer service representatives was designed to reduce customer complaints. Applying the skills and knowledge learned from the program resulted in a reduction in complaints, and the value of a single customer complaint was needed to determine the value of the improvement. Although customer service representatives had knowledge of some issues involved in customer complaints, they were not well versed in the full impact, so their supervisors were asked to provide a value.

In other situations, supervisors are asked to review and approve participants' estimates. After program completion, participants estimate the value of the improvements that are directly related to their own participation in the program. Their immediate managers are then asked to review the estimates and the process used by participants to arrive at the final estimates. Supervisors may confirm, adjust, or discard the values provided by the participants.

A key concern in the use of estimates is ensuring that the person providing the estimate has a clear picture of the full impact of the measure. In some cases, the participants' immediate supervisor has a better picture of the impact. For example, evaluation of a program in a call center required a value for the cost of one call escalation. The participants in the program to reduce call escalations were also the individuals who escalated calls to a higher level. While participants were the ones who made the decision to escalate a call, they sometimes were unaware of the consequences of the escalation for those at the next level. However, their immediate supervisor was in an excellent position to determine the value of eliminating an escalated call. The value was likely to include the cost of the supervisor's time and the cost of having a more disgruntled customer. At any rate, the supervisor would be a more credible source than the participants for the value in question.

Using Estimates from Senior Management

In rare cases, senior management provides estimates of a measure's value. In this approach, senior managers interested in the process or program are asked to place a value on the improvement based on their perception of its worth. This approach is used in situations in which calculating the value is difficult or in which other sources of estimation are unavailable or unreliable.

Here is an example of the use of supervisor estimates to assign a monetary value to a measure. A hospital chain was attempting to improve customer satisfaction through a program for all employees. The program was designed to improve customer service and, therefore, to improve the external customer satisfaction index. To determine the value of the program, a value for the unit of improvement (one point on the index) was needed. Because senior managers were interested in improving the index, they were asked to provide input on the value of a one-point increase. In a regular executive staff meeting, each senior manager and hospital administrator was asked to describe what it means for a hospital when the index increases.

After some discussion, each individual was asked to provide an estimate of the monetary value gained when the index moved one point. Although the senior managers were initially reluctant to provide the information, after some encouragement, monetary values were provided, adjusted for error, totaled, and averaged. The result was an estimate of the worth of one unit of improvement, which was used as a basis for calculating the benefits of the program. Although this process was subjective, it had the advantage of being owned by the senior executives—the same executives who approved the program budget.

Using Staff Estimates

The final method for converting data to monetary values is the use of staff estimates. Using all the available information as well as their experience, the staff members most familiar with the program provide estimates of the value of improvement. For example, an international oil company created a dispatcher training program in order to reduce dispatcher absenteeism and other performance problems. The staff estimated the cost of an absence to be $200. This value was then used to calculate the savings represented by the reduction in absenteeism that followed the training of the dispatchers. Although the staff may be capable of providing accurate estimates, this approach may be perceived as biased. In this case, for example, the staff might want the value of each absence to be large so that the savings generated by the program they created will be impressive. Therefore, staff should be used to estimate the monetary value of a measure only when other approaches are not possible.

Final Thoughts

This brief chapter discusses the method of last resort for converting data to monetary values: using estimates from the most knowledgeable and credible sources. The likely choices to provide estimates are the participants in the program, the immediate manager of the participants, and managers at other levels. In addition, the staff members involved in developing the program may provide estimates.

Credibility is the key issue in obtaining estimates of monetary values. If credibility becomes a problem in evaluating measures of improvement, there is an alternative. If data cannot be converted to monetary values credibly and with minimum resources, then they are left as intangible measures. Intangible measures are covered in Chapter Seven. Now that we have presented techniques to convert measures to monetary value, it is important to review some issues involved with the use of these techniques. This discussion is presented in Chapter Six.

6

Use of Data Conversion Techniques

This book has presented a variety of ways to convert data to monetary values. Sometimes, choosing the best method can be confusing. This chapter focuses on the use of the techniques, exploring some of the issues that must be addressed for successful and consistent practice within the ROI Methodology.

Selecting the Appropriate Technique

When so many techniques for data conversion are available, it can be challenging to select one or more techniques appropriate to the situation. The guidelines in this section can help you determine the proper method.

Use the technique that is appropriate for the type of data. Some techniques are designed specifically for hard data, while others are more appropriate for soft data. Therefore, the type of data will often dictate the technique. Hard data, while always preferred, are not always available. Soft data are often required and must be addressed through techniques that are appropriate for soft data. For example, hard data such as quality measures often have standard values. Soft data measures such as employee satisfaction can be converted to money by linking them with customer satisfaction.

Move from the most accurate technique to the least accurate. The techniques in this book are presented in order of accuracy and credibility, beginning with the most credible. Using standard, accepted values is the most credible method; staff estimates are the least credible. Work down the list, considering the feasibility of each technique, given the situation. Use of the technique with the most accuracy and credibility is recommended.

Consider availability and convenience. Sometimes, the availability of a particular method will drive the selection. In other situations, the convenience of a technique may be an important factor in making a selection.

For estimates, use the source with the broadest perspective—the person who knows the measure and its value best. To improve the accuracy of an estimate, the broadest possible perspective on the issue is needed. The individual providing an estimate must be knowledgeable on all the processes and issues involved in the value of the data item.

Use multiple techniques when feasible. Sometimes, using more than one technique to obtain a value is helpful. When multiple sources are readily available, more than one source should be used, for comparison or to provide another perspective. When multiple sources are used, the data must be integrated by applying a rule, such as using the lowest value, which is a preferred approach because it is the conservative choice. (This approach follows Guiding Principle 4: When analyzing data, select the most conservative alternative for calculations.)

The most conservative approach yields the lowest ROI. Therefore, if benefits are under consideration, remember that benefits are in the numerator of the ROI equation, so selecting the lowest value will yield the lowest ROI.

Minimize the amount of time. As in other processes, keeping the time invested as low as possible is important, so that the total time and effort for the evaluation does not become excessive. Some techniques can be implemented in less time than others. This step in the ROI Methodology can quickly absorb more time than all the other steps combined. Too much time spent on this step may dampen enthusiasm for the process and increase total program costs.

Ensuring the Accuracy and Credibility of Data

Credibility: The Key Issue

The techniques presented in this book assume that each data item collected and linked with a program can be converted to a monetary value. Although estimates can be developed using one or more of these techniques, the process of converting data to monetary values may lose credibility with the target audience, who may doubt its use in the analysis. Very subjective data, such as a change in employee morale or a reduction in the number of employee conflicts, are difficult to convert to monetary values. The key question in this determination is "Could these results be presented to senior management with confidence?" If the process does not meet this credibility test, the data should not be converted to monetary values and instead should be listed as an intangible benefit. Other data, especially hard data items, can be used in the ROI calculation, leaving the very subjective data as intangibles.

When it is unclear whether a data item should be converted, use the four-part test shown in Figure 6.1. Note the importance of the final question: "Can we convince our executive in two minutes that the value is credible?" This is the ultimate reality test, for time is limited when results are communicated to management. If buy-in is not achieved quickly, then the credibility of the entire process may be questioned.

When converting data to a monetary value, it is important to be consistent and methodical in your approach. Specific rules for making conversions will ensure this consistency and, ultimately, enhance the reliability of the study. Using the Guiding Principles will help with this issue.

Figure 6.1. Four-Part Test for Data Conversion

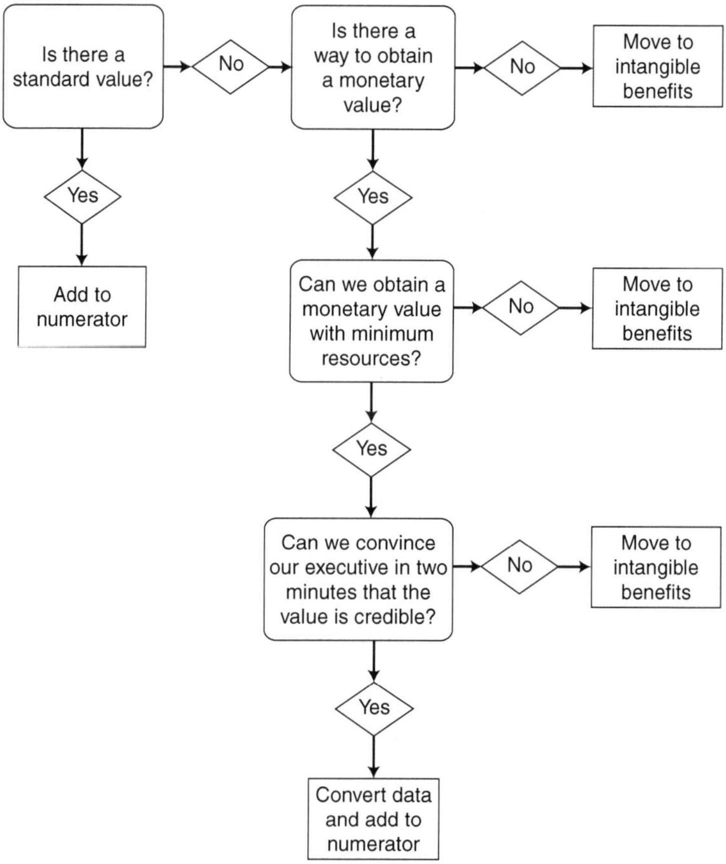

The accuracy of data and the credibility of the data conversion process are important concerns, causing some professionals to avoid converting data to monetary values. They are more comfortable reporting, for example, that a program reduced absenteeism from 6 percent to 4 percent, without attempting to place a value on the improvement. They assume that each person receiving the information will place a value on the reduction in absenteeism. Unfortunately, the target audience may know little about the cost of absenteeism and may underestimate the actual value of the improvement. Because stakeholders may undervalue the benefits of a program, some attempt should be made to include data conversion in the ROI analysis.

How the Credibility of Data Is Influenced

When ROI data are presented to selected target audiences, its credibility will be an issue. The degree to which the target audience believes the data are credible will be influenced by many factors. Credibility issues surface during the isolation step, during which estimates are sometimes used to isolate the effects of the program, and during data conversion, when estimates are used as well.

Completing an exercise on the credibility of data may be helpful. Exhibit 6.1 presents seven data items. Each item is presented as fact, and individuals are asked to believe each one. They represent annual values and the source of the item is included. Take a few minutes to indicate which of these items are the most credible by ranking them from 1 to 7, with 1 being the most credible and 7 being the least credible.

Next, for each item, list the factors that make it credible and the factors that make it not so credible. Essentially, the purpose of this exercise is to understand what makes people believe data. This is sometimes an eye-opening exercise, because it shows that many factors can affect credibility.

Exhibit 6.1. How Credible Are These Data Items?

	Rank
1. The cumulative expenditure on child sex abuse claims in the United States for the Roman Catholic Church is $1.5 billion. *Source:* U.S. Conference of Catholic Bishops.	☐
2. Vulcan Materials Company produced 275 million tons of crushed stone during the year. *Source:* Vulcan Materials Company Annual Report, audited by Deloitte & Touche.	☐

Exhibit 6.1. How Credible Are These Data Items? (*Continued*)

	Rank
3. A pharmaceutical firm in Ireland received a –42% ROI (negative) in a management training program. *Source:* Jack J. Phillips and Patti P. Phillips (eds.), *ROI at Work*, Alexandria, Va.: American Society for Training and Development.	☐
4. Wachovia Bank received a 932% ROI in a training program for relationship managers. *Source:* Patti P. Phillips (ed.), *In Action: Measuring Return on Investment,* Vol. 3. Alexandria, Va.: American Society for Training and Development.	☐
5. The annual cost of absenteeism and diminished productivity resulting from employee depression is $23.8 billion. *Source:* Massachusetts Institute of Technology study, reported in *Nation's Business.*	☐
6. The annual value of the market for wildlife trafficking—the second largest illegal trade in the world after drugs—is $10 billion. *Source:* U.S. Department of State.	☐
7. Presenteeism (working while sick) is costing employers $15 billion each year.	☐

Source: The Today Show, NBC.

Here are a few comments about these data items.

1. This item about the Roman Catholic Church is suspect because the church has not been forthcoming in addressing the issue of sex abuse. Some may not believe the value, suggesting that it could be understated.

2. This example from Vulcan Materials seems to be specific and is often rated as the most credible item. However, note that the data item presented here is not shipments to customers but

production. The company measures its shipments to customers but does not measure the crushed rock produced. Instead, an estimation process based on the concept of inventory adjustment is used. If the inventory at the end of the year is the same from one year to the next, then the customer shipments equaled the production. However, if the inventory goes up when compared to the customer shipments, which are known, the production equals the customer shipments plus the adjustment. To measure the inventory, an airplane flies over the quarry, allowing an individual in the plane to estimate the circumference of the rock piles, from which the volume of the piles and then the weight of the stone in inventory can be estimated. This appears to be an accurate number, yet it includes error. It is an estimate. Operating managers are also allowed to make minor adjustments in the inventory values based on the idea that they may know more about the amount of stone in inventory than the estimation reveals. In summary, the figure that is reported in the financial documents is at best a rough estimate of the amount of production. It suffices for the company, but it seems more credible than it actually is.

3. This item usually receives high credibility marks. Respondents reason that if a firm is willing to present a negative ROI, then the ROI must not be biased and might be accurate.

4. This often gets low marks because the ROI seems unrealistic or unbelievable. Also, the method used to arrive at the number is questionable. If the method described in the cited book was used, then it may be credible. If not, perhaps it is not so credible.

5. Several issues are raised in this item. First, the method for connecting absenteeism and productivity due to depression is a major issue. Obviously, it would be impossible to go to employers and find this information, because the specific reason for an absence is not usually recorded. If the data are clinical—that is, if employees have been diagnosed as clinically depressed—limited information may be obtained from the employees about the

number of absences caused by depression and the approximate productivity lost for this reason. However, the number may still be hard to believe.

Another issue, which is not apparent in the statement, is that this study was funded by a pharmaceutical firm that manufactures a drug to treat depression. Also this study was reported in a business publication and not in a medical journal.

6. This data item brings up issues about its source and how the number was determined.

7. This item also raises issues about its source and the method used to determine the number.

What does all this mean? The second part of the exercise begins to identify some issues that can affect the credibility of data or an individual's perception of the credibility.

Rules for Determining Credibility

The previous exercise can be summarized by the issues shown in Exhibit 6.2, which are the major influences on credibility. The

Exhibit 6.2. The Major Influences on Credibility

- Reputation of the data source

- Reputation of the study source

- Motives of the evaluators

- Personal biases of the audience

- Methodology of the study

- Assumptions made during the analysis

- Realism of the outcome data

- Type of data

- Scope of the analysis

concerns about the data set presented in the exercise can usually be categorized as one of these influences.

Reputation of the Source of the Data

The source of the data represents the first credibility issue. How credible are the individuals or the groups providing the data? Do they understand the issues? Are they knowledgeable about all the processes? Are they biased? The target audience will often give more credibility to data obtained from those who are closest to the source of the improvement or change.

Reputation of the Source of the Study

The target audience scrutinizes the reputation of the individuals, groups, or organizations that present the data. Do they have a history of providing accurate reports? Are they unbiased in their analyses? Are they fair in their presentation? Answers to these and other questions will help the audience form an impression about the source's reputation.

Motives of the Evaluators

The audience will look for motives of the person or persons conducting the study. Do the individuals presenting the data have a motive for exaggerating the results? Do they have a personal interest in creating a favorable or unfavorable result? Do they claim "ownership" of the program or part of it? Are the stakes high if the study is unfavorable? The audience will examine these and other issues in order to determine motives.

Audience Bias

The audience may have a bias—positive or negative—toward a particular study or toward the data presented from the study. Some executives may have a positive feeling about a program and will need fewer data to convince them of its value. Other executives may have a negative attitude toward the program and will need more data in order to be convinced of the data's accuracy. The potential bias of the audience should be understood early so that the presentation can be designed to counter any biases.

Methodology of the Study

The audience will want to know specifically how the research was conducted. How were the calculations made? What steps were followed? What processes were used? A lack of information about the methodology will cause the audience to become wary and suspicious of the results. Audience members will substitute their own perceptions and conclusions about the methodology if information is not provided.

Assumptions Made During the Analysis

The audience will try to understand the basis for the analysis. What definitions are used? What are the assumptions in the evaluation? Are they standard? How do they compare with assumptions in other studies? When assumptions are omitted, the audience members will substitute their own, often-unfavorable assumptions. In studies using the ROI Methodology, the conservative Twelve Guiding Principles are used in performing calculations and arriving at conclusions, in order to maximize credibility.

Realism of the Outcome Data

When outcomes appear to be unrealistic, the target audience may have difficulty believing them. Huge claims often fall on deaf ears, causing reports to be thrown away before they are reviewed. Impressive ROI values could cause problems.

Type of Data

Members of the target audience will usually have a preference for hard data. They are seeking business performance data tied to output, quality, costs, and time. These measures are easily understood and closely related to organizational performance. Conversely, soft data are sometimes viewed suspiciously from the outset; many senior executives will be concerned about their soft nature and the limitations of analysis of soft data.

Scope of Analysis

Do the data represent one organization or many? The smaller the scope, the more credible the data. Is the scope of the analysis narrow? Does it involve just one group or all the employees in the organization? Limiting the study to a small group or a small series of groups makes the process more accurate and believable.

How to Address the Issue of Credibility

The factors listed in the preceding section will influence the credibility of an ROI impact study and provide a framework from which to develop the ROI report. Therefore, in addition to considering each of the factors, consider the following key points when you are developing an ROI impact study for presentation to senior management.

Use the Most Credible and Reliable Sources for Estimates

This fundamental principle (Guiding Principle 3) must be addressed throughout an ROI evaluation, and therefore, it has been consistently discussed throughout these books. In some cases, the program participants are the most credible source, particularly when the evaluator is attempting to isolate the effects of the program. However, when the evaluator is converting data to monetary values, a higher-level manager may be more credible because he or she may have a broader view of the issues.

Remain Unbiased and Objective

This is a difficult issue, but it must be addressed. In an ideal setting, the person conducting the evaluation does not own the program. The ideal situation does occur in some organizations—evaluators are independent of the program's design, development, and delivery and of any other forms of ownership. When this ideal cannot be achieved, other methods are often available to help with credibility.

During data collection, the credibility issue may surface. If the person collecting the data wanted to influence the results of the evaluation, the data could be adjusted in a variety of ways. Negative data could be eliminated, neutral data could be made positive, and positive data could be enhanced. While this scenario may seem improbable, it does happen. Therefore, the data collection needs to be as independent as possible.

A variety of options can help build the credibility of the data:

1. A person or group within the organization (for example, a colleague, the finance and accounting department, or the organizational effectiveness unit) may agree to collect the data. The data are then included in the report in a summarized form. The audience should be informed that the data collection was independent.

2. Sometimes when data are collected by electronic means, the independence is built into the process. The data go to a server, and the server sends a data summary. The raw data are never visible to the evaluator.

3. In other situations, a person or small firm specializing in evaluation will agree to collect data, summarize it, and return it at a low cost.

4. External consultants are readily available to collect the data, analyze it, and report it.

5. If none of the preceding options is available, then the issue should be addressed early in the communication. The audience should understand at the beginning that the person conducting the study also owns the program, and it should be stated that the data were not changed or altered in any way and that a summary of the data is contained in an appendix of the report.

Prepare for Potential Audience Bias

Preparation involves understanding the audience who will receive the report or be present during the meeting in which the study is presented. Audiences sometimes have biases. When the biases are understood, preparation to address those biases becomes important. Ideally, addressing the issues that might feed audience biases would be an effective strategy. Ensuring that efforts are made to moderate negative and positive bias is important.

Fully Explain Your Methodology at Each Step in the Process

An explanation of methodology is important because understanding the method used to capture and analyze the data leads to an understanding of the data's credibility. In this context, the audience must understand that a systematic, accepted method has been used, with logical steps and sequences, and that there were options along the way. This is sometimes helpful when executives and audience members want to know whether a proven method was used to convert the data to monetary values.

Define Assumptions Made During the Analysis

Assumptions are critical. They need to be logical and, most of all, conservative. In the ROI Methodology, the assumptions are the Guiding Principles, which are listed in the section titled "Principles of the ROI Methodology" at the beginning of this book. They become an evaluator's best friend when the evaluator is dealing with credibility issues. Conservative assumptions help increase the credibility of the process.

Prepare for an Unrealistic Value

In a sense, this is a good problem to have. If the ROI number is high, which for some people would be good news, the challenge is to make the audience believe the number. Executives, managers, and chief financial officers are used to ROI values in the range of

15 to 20 percent. If ten or twenty times this amount is reported, it may be difficult for them to believe the figure.

Two issues must be underscored. First, if the conservative Twelve Guiding Principles of the ROI Methodology are used, the value that is being presented is an understatement of the results, so the ROI is even greater than the value reported. Second, it is possible and sometimes routine for successful programs to drive high ROIs. This phenomenon is explored in more detail in the next book in the series, *Costs and ROI*. Essentially, this is the leverage effect. That is, spending money on one group of individuals can have an effect on a larger group. This is particularly true in a program such as executive development in which a change in an executive's behavior can affect the entire department, division, region, or company under that executive's influence. As a result, investing in one person can have a multiplicative effect.

Finally, performing sensitivity analysis may be helpful. That is, the audience needs to know that if some assumptions were changed and made even more conservative, the value would be different. The audience needs to understand that while the figure is high, it is probably less than what has actually been achieved. Depending on the assumptions made, the figure could be higher or lower; however, the figure reported is based on conservative assumptions.

Use Hard Data Whenever Possible

If an evaluation includes an ROI calculation, then the data are converted to monetary values and those are the hard data—and are tangible. If soft data are involved, an attempt should be made to convert these data to monetary values. If they are converted, then they have become tangible. However, some data will not be converted, and they will remain intangible. Every effort should be made to convert the data to monetary values.

Executives prefer the data to be hard data. When soft data are converted, credibility will be an issue. Are they credible data? See if they meet the credibility test shown in Figure 6.1. An important point, however, is that intangible benefits are still important, as the next chapter explains.

Keep the Scope of Analysis Narrow

The narrower the scope, the more credible the evaluation. This means that an ROI evaluation is more credible when it is conducted on one program than it is when it is conducted on multiple programs and more credible when it involves one group of employees rather than all the employees in the company. It is not as credible when an entire function is subjected to the evaluation—for example, when the effort is to calculate the payoff of the entire learning and development function or the whole technology budget.

In conclusion, these guidelines provide rules for presenting data credibly. Credibility is king when ROI studies are communicated. Credibility issues must be acknowledged and addressed at each step in order to maintain high credibility with the target audience and to collect believable data.

Making Adjustments

Consider the Possibility of Management Adjustment

In organizations in which soft data are common and values are derived through imprecise methods, senior managers and administrators are sometimes offered the opportunity to review and approve the data. Because of the subjective nature of this process, management may wish to factor out parts of the data in order to make the final results more credible.

This approach is not recommended, because there is no valid reason to do this on a routine basis. However, if the management team members who support and sponsor programs need to make an adjustment in order to accept the data, evaluators should allow them to do it formally. If evaluators don't allow it, the management team may do it anyway.

Consider the Issue of Short-Term Versus Long-Term Programs

When data are converted to monetary values, usually one year of data is included in the analysis. This practice follows Guiding Principle 9, which states that for short-term solutions, only the first-year benefits are used in the ROI analysis. However, some programs are long-term rather than short-term programs. Whether a program is short-term or long-term is defined by how long it takes to complete or implement the program. If one individual participating in the program and working through the process takes months to complete it, then it probably is not a short-term program. Some programs take years to implement with one particular group. A good rule of thumb is to consider a program short-term when an individual takes a month or less to learn what needs to be done to make the program successful.

When a program is long-term, the time period during which benefits will be assumed to accrue should be set before program evaluation. Input should be secured from all stakeholders, including the sponsor, champion, implementer, designer, and evaluator. After some discussion, the final estimate of the time period for program effects should be conservative and perhaps should be reviewed by finance and accounting. When a long-term solution is under consideration, forecasting will need to be used to estimate multiple years of value; no sponsor will wait several years to see how a program turns out. Some assumptions will need to be made so that the forecast can be completed.

Consider an Adjustment for the Time Value of Money

Since a program investment is made in one time period and the return is realized at a later time, some organizations adjust program benefits to reflect the time value of money by using discounted cash-flow techniques. The monetary benefits of the program are discounted on the basis of the time period between outlay and return. The amount of adjustment, however, is usually small compared with the typical benefits of programs.

Although the time value of money may not be an issue for every program, it should be considered, and some type of standard discount rate should be used. Consider an example of how this is calculated. A program cost of $100,000 and a two-year period will be used before the full value of the investment will be covered. (This is a long-term solution spanning two years.) Using a discount rate of 6 percent, the adjusted cost for the program for the first year would be $100,000 \times 106\% = \$106,000$. For the second year it would be $106,000 \times 106\% = \$112,360$. Therefore, the program cost has been adjusted for a two-year value with a 6 percent discount rate. This calculation assumes that the program sponsor could have invested the money in some other program and obtained at least a 6 percent return on that investment; hence another cost has been added to the program cost.

Converting Data to Money: Matching Exercise

As a review of the techniques for converting data to monetary values, we have provided a matching exercise. This exercise will serve as a reminder of the methods described in this book.

This exercise shows the versatility of the methods for converting data to monetary values. The good news is that many credible methods are available. Some are easy to use, and most of the values have already been developed. Even better news is that if the data

---

Instructions

For each of the following situations, please indicate the method used to convert data to monetary values. Select from these methods:

A. Profit or savings from output (standard value)
B. Cost of quality (standard value)
C. Employee time as compensation (standard value)
D. Historical costs or savings from records
E. Expert input
F. External database
G. Linking with other measures
H. Participant estimation
 I. Management estimation
J. Staff estimation

In each box, write the letter that corresponds to the method used.

Situation	Conversion Technique
1. The Veteran's Administration was experiencing a high turnover rate among its nurses. A new human resources program was designed to reduce turnover. To obtain the value of one voluntary turnover, the Internet was used to find a health care study that showed the average cost (fully loaded) of replacing a nurse. This number, expressed as a percentage of salary, was used in the calculation.	☐
2. A new program for couriers at DHL was designed to reduce the number of repackaging errors. A repackaging error occurs when a package is damaged by the couriers and has to be repackaged before delivery. The quality office in Brussels had previously determined the standard cost for a repackaging error. This amount was used to develop the total monetary value for the reduction in errors.	☐

Situation	Conversion Technique
3. Middle-level managers at an electric utility were involved in a time management program. Each manager estimated the number of hours saved each week that were directly attributable to this program. The value calculated for each hour saved was based on the average annual salary of the managers, adjusted for employee benefits and divided by the number of hours worked in one year to reach an hourly cost.	☐
4. An Australian government agency was implementing a new human resources program to reduce the number of stress claims filed by employees. The employees, who worked with angry and upset people, were suffering from extreme stress on the job, resulting in many claims. To obtain the monetary value of a stress claim, medical and health staff provided an average value for one claim based on their expertise in managing stress claims for several years.	☐
5. A new customer call center program at a home appliance company was designed to reduce the number of calls that were escalated to the next level of management. The individuals involved in the program were the immediate supervisors of the employees taking the calls. To determine the cost of a call escalation, the participants (supervisors) estimated the cost attached to one escalated call.	☐
6. A pharmaceutical company was implementing a new ethics program for all employees. While several outcomes were expected from this program, one performance measure was expense account violations. To obtain the average cost of an expense account violation, the cost of all of the	☐

Situation	Conversion Technique

violations for a two-month period was taken
directly from the records and divided by the total
violations.

7. Employee engagement data were collected for a
   global computer company. After the data were
   analyzed, a new human resources program was
   designed in order to improve engagement scores.
   To place a value on a change in engagement
   score, the staff examined the correlation between
   engagement scores and employee turnover in
   different job groups. This correlation analysis was
   easily performed as part of the company's human
   capital management system. As engagement
   scores improved, voluntary turnover decreased.
   The cost savings from the corresponding
   turnover reduction was used as the value for
   each change in the engagement score.

8. A small equipment manufacturing company was
   interested in reducing absenteeism. A program
   was implemented, and the cost of one absence
   was needed in order to calculate the monetary
   impact. The human resources staff member who
   conducted the study estimated the cost of one
   absence to be $300 per day.

9. A major retail store chain was anxious to reduce
   the number of customer complaints that it
   received. A new program was implemented for
   that purpose; naturally, the cost of a complaint
   was needed in order to evaluate the program. To
   obtain the cost of one complaint, the
   management of the customer service area and
   the vice president of customer care estimated the
   average cost of one complaint.

Situation	Conversion Technique
10. Wachovia Bank implemented an advanced negotiation program in which commercial bankers learned how to increase revenue from new and existing clients. The outcome of the program was increased revenue in specific product lines. To calculate the monetary value of a sale, the revenue amount was multiplied by the profit margin for the product line, which was considered a standard value in the organization.	☐

Responses

1. **F**. In this example, the evaluator used the Internet to find a value for turnover in a particular setting, health care, and a particular job group, nursing. This should be a credible value.

2. **B**. This is a standard value located in the quality department. It is an accepted value that has already been calculated and used for this measure. This conversion is credible.

3. **C**. This example uses a standard value for time. The cost per hour of manager time is not an estimate of the value. In the example, the time is an estimate, but the value is a standard value that reflects fully loaded compensation—salary plus benefits.

4. **E**. The medical staff are experts who can provide a credible value for the measure in question.

5. **H**. In this example, the value for one escalated call is obtained directly from the program participants. The credibility of this value will rest on the participants' understanding of the full scope of this measure—that is, how well they know and understand the issue.

6. **D**. While this method is credible, it is very time-consuming. Adding all the expense account violations and dividing by the number of violations takes a large amount of resources and time.

7. **G**. This method can be credible if the correlation analysis is credible. The important issue is that the data were developed with the input of someone outside the owners of the program. A calculation was not performed by the staff for this program. If the staff had had to develop the value, it would have taken too much time.

8. **J**. This is perhaps the least credible data conversion because the human resources staff has a stake in the value of one absence being large because it affects the ROI. This method of estimating the value of a measure is not recommended, except as a last resort, and even then, it may not meet the credibility test when the program evaluation is presented to management. The measure may have to be left as intangible.

9. **I**. The credibility of the value rests on the credibility of the managers who provided it. They may well be in a good position to place a monetary value on this item.

10. **A**. This method is very credible. The example uses a standard value profit margin for the product.

---

cannot be converted to a monetary value, the measure can be left as an intangible. The next chapter discusses intangible measures in detail.

Final Thoughts

This chapter provides a quick review of the data conversion methods in this book and discusses several issues involved in their use. When conversion is attempted, the most critical issue is credibility, and the second most important issue is the required resources. These two issues must be considered in tandem; the conversion may take too much time and effort, and it could lose credibility. The final chapter in this book covers intangible measures, the measures that cannot be or are not converted to monetary values.

7

Intangible Measures

Program results usually include both tangible and intangible measures. Intangible measures represent the benefits or detriments directly linked to a program that cannot or should not be converted to monetary values. By definition, according to Guiding Principle 11 of the ROI Methodology, an intangible measure is one that is purposely not converted to a monetary value. (If a conversion cannot be accomplished with minimum resources and with credibility, the measure is considered an intangible.) Intangible measures are often monitored after the program has been implemented. Although they are not converted to monetary values, intangible measures are nonetheless an important part of the evaluation process. This chapter explores the role of intangibles, how to measure them, when to measure them, and how to report them.

The range of intangible measures is almost limitless. Exhibit 7.1 highlights over two dozen examples of these measures. Some measures make the list because of the difficulty in measuring them; others because of the difficulty in converting them to money. Others are on the list for both reasons. Being labeled as intangible does not mean that these items can never be measured or converted to monetary values. In one study or another, each of these items has been monitored and quantified in financial terms. However, in typical programs, these measures are considered intangible benefits

Exhibit 7.1. Common Intangibles

• Accountability	• Innovation and creativity
• Alliances	• Job satisfaction
• Attention	• Leadership
• Awards	• Loyalty
• Branding	• Networking
• Capability	• Organizational commitment
• Capacity	• Partnering
• Clarity	• Reputation
• Communication	• Stress
• Corporate social responsibility	• Sustainability
• Customer service (customer satisfaction)	• Team effectiveness
• Employee attitudes	• Timeliness
• Engagement	• Work/life balance
• Image	

because of the difficulty in measuring them or the difficulty in converting them to monetary values.

Why Intangibles Are Important

Although intangible measures are not new, they are becoming increasingly important. Intangibles secure funding and drive the economy, and organizations are built on them. Everywhere we look, intangibles are becoming not only increasingly important but also critical to organizations. Here's a recap of why they have become so important.

Intangibles Are the Invisible Advantage

When the elements behind the success of many well-known organizations are examined, intangibles are often found. A highly innovative company continues to develop new and improved products; a government agency reinvents itself; a company with highly involved and engaged employees attracts and keeps talent. A large consulting firm shares knowledge with employees, providing a competitive advantage. Still another organization is successful because of its strategic partners and alliances. These intangibles do not often appear in cost statements or other records, but they are there, and they make a huge difference.

Trying to identify, measure, and react to intangibles may be difficult, but it is possible to do so. Intangibles transform the way organizations work, the way employees are managed, the way products are designed, the way services are sold, and the way customers are treated. The implications are profound, and an organization's strategy must address them. Although they are invisible, the presence of intangibles is felt and the results of their presence are concrete.

We Are Entering the Intangible Economy

Our economy has been constantly changing since before the Iron Age. One of the biggest changes was the transition to the agricultural age. In the late nineteenth century and early twentieth century, the world took another leap forward, moving into the industrial age. From the 1950s on, the world has moved into the technology and knowledge age; this evolution translates into an emphasis on intangibles.

During all of these changes, a natural evolution of technology has occurred. During the industrial age, companies and individuals invested in tangible assets, like manufacturing plants and equipment. In the technology and knowledge age, companies invest in intangible assets, like brands or systems. The future will hold more of the same, as intangibles continue to evolve as an important part of the overall economic system (Boulton, Libert, and Samek, 2000).

Intangibles Are Being Converted to Tangibles

Data once regarded as intangible are now being converted into monetary values. As a result of this trend, once-classic intangibles are now accepted as tangible measures because their value is more easily understood. Consider, for example, customer satisfaction. Just a decade ago, few organizations had a clue about the monetary value of customer satisfaction. Now, more firms have taken the step of linking customer satisfaction directly to revenues and profits. Companies are seeing the tremendous value that can be derived from intangibles. As this chapter illustrates, more information is being accumulated in order to show monetary values for intangible data, moving some intangible measures into the tangible category.

Intangibles Drive Programs

Some programs are implemented because of intangibles. For example, the need to have greater collaboration, partnering, communication, teamwork, or better customer service drives new programs. In the public sector, the need to reduce poverty, employ disadvantaged citizens, and save lives often drives programs. From the outset, the intangibles are the important drivers and become the most important measures. Consequently, an increasing number of executives include a string of intangibles on their scorecards, reports on key performance indicators, dashboards, and other routine reporting systems. In some cases, the intangibles represent nearly half of all measures that are monitored.

Measuring Intangibles

In some programs, intangibles are more important than monetary measures and therefore should be monitored and reported as part of the evaluation. In practice, almost every program, regardless of its nature, scope, or content, produces intangible measures. The challenge is to identify them effectively and report them appropriately.

From time to time, it is necessary to explore the issue of measuring the difficult to measure. Responses to this exploration usually occur in the form of comments instead of questions. "You can't measure it" is a typical response. This is not true, because anything can be measured. What the frustrated observer suggests by that comment is that the intangible is not something you can count, examine, or see in quantities, like items produced on an assembly line. In reality, a quantitative value can be assigned to or developed for any intangible. If it exists, it can be measured. Consider human intelligence, for example. Although human intelligence is vastly complex and abstract, with myriad facets and qualities, IQ scores are assigned to many people, and most people seem to accept them. The software engineering institute at Carnegie-Mellon University assigns software organizations a score of 1 to 5 to represent their maturity in software engineering. This score has enormous implications for the organizations' business development capabilities, yet the measure goes practically unchallenged (Alden, 2006).

Several approaches to measuring intangibles are available. Intangibles that can be counted include customer complaints, employee complaints, and conflicts. These can be recorded easily and constitute one of the most acceptable types of measures for intangibles. Unfortunately, many intangibles are based on attitudes and perceptions that must be measured in order to provide a value. The key is in the development of the measurement instrument. Instruments are usually developed with scales of 3, 5, or even 10 points to represent levels of perception. The methods for measuring intangibles represent three basic varieties.

The first method is use of a survey instrument. One type of instrument lists the intangible items and asks respondents to agree or disagree on a 5-point scale (on which the midpoint represents a neutral opinion). Other instruments define various qualities of the intangible, such as its reputation. A 5-point scale can easily

Figure 7.1. The Link Between Hard-to-Measure and Easy-to-Measure Items

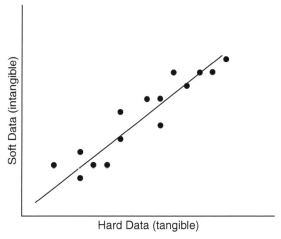

be developed to describe degrees of reputation, ranging from the worst rating (a horrible reputation) to the best rating (an excellent reputation). Still other instruments solicit ratings of agreement or disagreement on a scale of 1 to 10 after respondents review a description of the intangible.

A second way to measure an intangible connects it to a measure that is easier to measure or easier to value. As shown in Figure 7.1, a hard-to-measure item is linked to an easy-to-measure item. In the classic situation, a soft measure (typically the intangible) is connected to a hard measure (typically the tangible). Although this link can be developed through logical deductions and conclusions, gathering some empirical evidence through a correlation analysis (as shown in the figure) that demonstrates a significant correlation between the items is the best approach. However, a detailed analysis would have to be conducted to ensure the existence of a causal relationship between the items. In other words, just because a correlation is apparent, it does not mean that one caused the other. Consequently, additional analysis, other empirical evidence, and supporting data would be needed to provide evidence of a causal effect.

A final method of measuring an intangible is development of an index. An index is a single score representing some complex factor; it is constructed by aggregating the values of several different measures. These may be a combination of both hard and soft data items. Measures making up the index are sometimes weighted according to their importance as elements of the abstract factor being measured. Some index measures are based strictly on hard data items. For example, the U.S. poverty level is a family income equal to three times the cost of feeding a family of four as determined by the U.S. Department of Agriculture, adjusted for inflation using the consumer price index. Sometimes an index is completely intangible—for example, the customer satisfaction index developed by the University of Michigan.

Intangibles are often combined with a variety of tangibles to reflect the performance of a business unit or program. Intangibles are often associated with nonprofit, nongovernment, and public sector organizations. Table 7.1 shows the performance measures that reflect greatness at the Cleveland Orchestra. For the Cleveland Orchestra, intangibles include such items as comments from cab drivers; tangibles include ticket sales. Collectively and regardless of how difficult they are to obtain, these data sets reflect the overall performance of the orchestra.

Converting Intangibles to Monetary Values

Converting hard-to-measure data items to monetary values is challenging, to say the least. When working with intangibles, interest in the monetary contribution expands considerably compared to, for example, measures of productivity, where the monetary value can be more clearly interpreted. Three major groups have an interest in the monetary value of intangibles.

1. The sponsors who fund a particular program almost always seek monetary values among the measures.

Table 7.1. Measuring Greatness at the Cleveland Orchestra

Superior Performance	Distinctive Impact	Lasting Endurance
• Emotional response of audience; increase in number of standing ovations	• Cleveland's style of programming increasingly copied; becoming more influential	• Excellence sustained across generations of conductors—from George Szell through Pierre Boulez, Christoph von Dohnányi, and Franz Welser-Möst
• Wide technical range; can play any piece with excellence, no matter how difficult—from soothing and familiar classical pieces to difficult and unfamiliar modern pieces	• A key point of civic pride; cab drivers say, "We're really proud of our orchestra"	• Supporters donate time and money, invest in long-term success of orchestra; endowment tripled
• Increased demand for tickets; demand for more complex, imaginative programs in Cleveland, New York, and Europe	• Orchestra leaders increasingly sought for leadership roles and perspectives in elite industry groups and gatherings	
• Invited to Salzburg Festival (first time in twenty-five years), signifying elite status among top European orchestras		

Source: Adapted from Collins, 2005.

2. The public is involved in some way with many intangibles. Even private sector organizations are trying to improve their image, their reputation, and confidence in their organizations in the mind of the public.

3. The individuals who are actively involved with the program and who support it often need and sometimes demand that a monetary value be developed.

The path most commonly used to capture monetary values for intangibles is shown in Figure 7.2. The first challenge is to locate an existing value or to compute or measure the value in some way, making sure that the information is accurate and reliable. If it is not possible to locate an existing value, an expert may be able to assign a credible monetary value to the measure, based on his or her experience, knowledge, credentials, and track record. If an expert opinion is not available, stakeholders may provide their input, estimating the monetary value of the measure, although their estimates should be adjusted for bias. Some stakeholders are biased in one way or another; they may want the value to be smaller or larger, depending on their particular motives. Their estimates

Figure 7.2. Converting an Intangible Measure: Valuing the Hard-to-Value

Approach	Challenge
Existing data	Finding the right database
⇩	
Expert input	Locating a credible expert
⇩	
Stakeholder input	Making the data credible
⇩	
Analysis of data	Resources

may have to be adjusted or thrown out altogether. Finally, the data are converted, using conservative processes and adjusting for error as necessary. Unfortunately, no specific rule exists for converting each intangible measure to a monetary value. By definition, an intangible is a measure that is not converted to money. If the conversion cannot be accomplished with minimum resources and with credibility, it is left as an intangible.

Identifying and Collecting Intangibles

Intangible measures can be taken from different sources and at different times during the program life cycle, as depicted in Figure 7.3. They can be uncovered early in the process, during the needs assessment, and their collection can be planned as part of the overall data collection strategy. For example, one program might have several hard data measures linked to it. Job stress, an intangible measure, is also identified and monitored, with no plans to convert it to a monetary value. From the beginning, this measure is destined to be a nonmonetary, intangible benefit that is reported along with the ROI results.

Figure 7.3. Identifying Intangible Measures During the Program Life Cycle

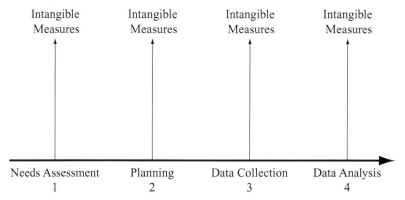

A second opportunity to identify intangible benefits is during the planning process, when clients or sponsors of the program agree on an evaluation plan. Key stakeholders can usually identify the intangible measures they expect to be influenced by the program. For example, a change management program in a large multinational company was conducted, and an ROI analysis was planned. Program leaders, participants, participants' managers, and experts identified potential intangible measures that were perceived to be influenced by the program, including collaboration, communication, and teamwork.

A third opportunity to collect intangible measures presents itself during data collection. Although the measure may not be anticipated in the initial design, it may surface on a questionnaire, in an interview, or during a focus group. Questions are often asked about other improvements linked to a program, and participants usually provide several intangible measures for which no plans are available for assigning a value. For example, in the evaluation of one program, participants were asked what specifically had improved about their work area and their relationships with customers as a result of the program. Participants provided more than a dozen intangible benefits that managers attributed to the program.

The fourth opportunity to identify intangible measures is during data analysis, while attempting to convert data to monetary values. If the conversion loses credibility, the measure should be reported as an intangible benefit. For example, in one sales improvement program, customer satisfaction was identified early in the process as a measure of program success. Conversion to a monetary value was attempted, but it lacked accuracy and credibility. Consequently, customer satisfaction was reported as an intangible benefit.

Analyzing Intangibles

For each intangible measure identified, some evidence of its connection to the program must be shown. However, in many cases, no specific analysis is planned beyond tabulation of responses. Early attempts to quantify intangible data sometimes resulted in aborting the entire process, with no further data analysis being conducted. In some cases, isolating the effects of the program may be undertaken, using one or more of the methods outlined in *Isolation of Results*, book three of this series. This step is necessary when an evaluator needs to know the specific amount of change in the intangible measure that is linked to the program. Intangible data often reflect improvement. However, neither the precise amount of improvement nor the amount of improvement directly related to a program is always identified. Because the value of these data is not included in the ROI calculation, intangible measures are not normally used to justify another program or to justify continuing an existing program. A detailed analysis is not necessary. Intangible benefits are often viewed as additional evidence of the program's success and are presented as supportive qualitative data.

Confronting Intangibles

There are so many intangibles that addressing them appropriately can be difficult. Many advances have been made in measuring intangibles effectively and in converting them to monetary values. Of course, when they are converted to monetary values, they are no longer intangible; they are tangible. This issue is not easy, but progress is being made and will continue to be made. The next section covers four examples in which organizations focus on measuring intangibles in the public sector and the private sector. These measures include only a few of the examples listed in Exhibit 7.1.

Example 1: Customer Service

Because of the importance of building and improving customer service, related measures are typically monitored to track payoff. Several types of customer service programs have a direct influence on these measures. This metric makes our list because it is perceived as difficult to measure and to convert to monetary value. However,

Figure 7.4. **Customer Service Linkage: Awareness, Attitudes, and Usage**

Type	Measures	Typical Questions
Awareness ⇓	Awareness and knowledge	Have you heard of Brand X? What brand comes to mind when you think "luxury car"?
Attitudes ⇓	Beliefs and intentions	Is Brand X for me? On a scale of 1 to 5, is Brand X for young people?
Usage ⇓	Purchasing habits and loyalty	Did you use Brand X this week? What brand did you last buy?

Source: Adapted from Farris, Bendle, Pfeifer, and Ribstein, 2006.

in the last two decades, much progress has been made, and some of these measures are routinely considered tangible because they are converted to monetary values by using the methods described in this chapter. The technique of linking to other measures that is used in our example is the most common way in which intangible measures of customer service are converted to monetary values. This technique follows the sequence shown in Figure 7.4. The first step is to create awareness of a particular product, service, or brand. The next step is to develop attitudes that define the beliefs, opinions, and intentions in regard to the product, service, or brand, and lead to usage, the final step that confirms the purchasing habits and loyalty of the customer.

The important links between awareness, attitudes, and usage are ingrained in most marketing and promotion programs and processes and have led to a variety of measures that are becoming standard in the field. Table 7.2 shows intangibles associated with

Table 7.2. Customer Service Intangibles

Metric	Definition	Issues	Purpose
Awareness	Percentage of total population who are aware of a brand.	Is awareness prompted or unprompted?	Consideration of who has heard of the brand.
Top of mind	First brand to be considered.	May be subject to most recent advertising or experience.	Saliency of brand.
Knowledge	Percentage of population who know product, have recollection of its advertising.	Not a formal metric. Is knowledge prompted or unprompted?	Extent of familiarity with product beyond name recognition.
Beliefs	Customers' or consumers' view of product, generally captured via survey (responses, often through ratings on a scale).	Customers or consumers may hold beliefs with varying degrees of conviction.	Perception of brand by attribute.
Purchasing intentions	Probability of intention to purchase.	To estimate probability of purchase, aggregate and analyze ratings of stated intentions.	Measures pre-shopping disposition to purchase.
Willingness to recommend	Intention to recommend to potential new customer (generally measured by ratings on scale of 1 to 5).	Nonlinear in impact.	Shows strength of loyalty, potential impact on others.

Customer satisfaction	Customers' satisfaction with brand in general or with specific attributes (generally measured on scale of 1 to 5).	Subject to response bias; captures views of current customers, not lost customers; satisfaction is a function of expectations.	Indicates likelihood of repurchase; reports of dissatisfaction show aspects requiring improvement to enhance loyalty.
Willingness to search	Percentage of customers willing to delay purchases, change stores, or reduce quantities to avoid switching brands.	Hard to capture.	Indicates importance of distribution coverage.
Loyalty	Customers' willingness to pay premium, to search, to stay.	"Loyalty" itself is not a formal metric, but specific metrics do measure aspects of this dynamic. New product entries may alter loyalty levels.	Indicates base future revenue stream.

Source: Adapted from Farris, Bendle, Pfeifer, and Ribstein, 2006, p. 16.

customer service and underscores the array of possibilities, all aimed at developing awareness, attitudes, and usage. The most common intangible is customer satisfaction, which is generally measured on scales of 1 to 5, 1 to 7, or 1 to 10 (although other scales are used, too). A tremendous amount of research has been accumulated about the value of satisfied customers and the loss connected with dissatisfied customers. Using elaborate processes of decision tree analysis, probability theories, expected value, and correlations, organizations have developed detailed relationships between customer service intangibles and monetary values, showing that movement in sales and profits is connected to a variety of measures. The most important measure is customer satisfaction. Within an organization, a variety of specific measures can be developed, including customer response time, sensitivity to costs and pricing issues, and creativity with customer responses. Of particular importance is the matter of response time. Providing prompt customer service is critical for most organizations. Therefore, organizations monitor the time required to respond to specific customer service requests or problems. Although reducing response times is a common objective, this measure is not usually converted to a monetary value. Therefore, customer response time is usually reported as an important intangible measure.

Example 2: Innovation and Creativity

Innovation and creativity are related. Creative employees create innovative products, services, and solutions. In our knowledge- and technology-based economy, innovation and creativity are becoming important factors in organizations' success.

Innovation

Innovation is critical to most organizations. Just how important is innovation? Let's put it in perspective. If it were not for the intellectual curiosity of employees—thinking things through, trying out new ideas, and taking wild guesses in R&D labs across the country—the United States would have half the economy it has today. In a recent report on research and development, the American Association for the Advancement for Science estimated that as much as 50 percent of U.S. economic growth in the half century since the Fortune 500 came into existence is the result of advances in technology (Brown, 2004).

After a few years' retrenchment and cost cutting, senior executives from a variety of industries now share the conviction that innovation—the ability to define and create new products and services and quickly bring them to market—is an increasingly important source of competitive advantage. Executives are setting aggressive performance goals for their innovation and product development organizations, targeting 20 to 30 percent improvements in such areas as time to market, development cost, product cost, and customer value (Kandybihn and Kihn, 2004).

There is a vast disconnect between hope and reality, however. A recent survey of fifty companies conducted by Booz Allen Hamilton shows that companies are only marginally satisfied that their innovation organizations are delivering their maximum potential. Worse, executives say that only half the improvement efforts they launch end up meeting expectations. Several waves of improvement in innovation and product development have already substantially enhanced companies' ability to deliver differentiated, high-quality products to markets quickly and efficiently. However, the degree of success achieved has varied greatly among companies and among units within companies. The differences in success stem from the difficulty in managing change in the complex processes and organizations associated with innovation and product development.

Some companies have managed to assemble an integrated "innovation chain" that is truly global and that allows them to outflank competitors that innovate using knowledge in a single cluster. They have been able to implement a process for innovating that transcends local clusters and national boundaries, becoming metanational innovators. This strategy of using localized pockets of technology, market intelligence, and human capabilities has provided a powerful new source of competitive advantage: more high-value innovation at lower cost (Santos, Doz, and Williamson, 2004).

Innovation is both easy and difficult to measure. Measuring outcomes in areas such as new products and processes, improved products and processes, copyrights, patents, inventions, and employee suggestions is easy. Many companies track these items. They can be documented in order to reflect the innovative profile of an organization. Unfortunately, comparing these data with previous data or benchmarking with other organizations is sometimes meaningless because these measures are typically unique to each organization and may not provide an accurate point of reference by which to gauge success.

Perhaps the most obvious way to measure innovation is by tracking patents—both those used internally and those licensed for others' use through a patent and license exchange. For example, IBM has been granted more patents than any other company in the world—more than 25,000 U.S. patents. IBM's licensing of patents and technology generates several billion dollars in profits each year. IBM and Microsoft are at the top of the list, but most organizations in the new economy monitor trademarks, patents, and copyrights as important measures of the innovative talent of their employees.

It is helpful to remember that the registration of patents stems from employees' inventive spirit. This means that employees do not have to be highly degreed scientists or engineers to be inventive. Although invention is often thought of in the context of technology, computing, materials, or energy, in fact it spans all disciplines and can therefore be extracted from any technological realm for application to problems in any area (Schwartz, 2004).

Through the years, inventors have been viewed as nerds, with much of their inventiveness explained by the quirky makeup of their personality. This image is popular because history is laced with well-known inventors endowed with an eccentric personality. In fact, however, inventors are usually ordinary people who possess extraordinary imagination. Many modern organizations of wide-ranging focus are devoting resources to the encouragement of employee creativity, from which they hope to gain advantages over their competition. Organizations intent on sparking ingenuity will consider innovation, monitor it, and take action to enhance it.

BusinessWeek uses a widely recognized evaluation process to develop its annual list of the world's most innovative companies (McGregor, 2006). This list of companies that have produced the top twenty-five innovations of the year is both comprehensive and respected. In partnership with Boston Consulting Group, the evaluation begins with a survey of innovation distributed electronically to executives worldwide early in the year, targeting 1,500 global corporations (determined by market capitalization). The executives are instructed to distribute the survey to their top ten executives. The survey is also accessible on several Web sites. The survey consists of nineteen general questions on innovation, as well as questions that focus on innovation metrics. In 2006, Apple, Google, 3M, Toyota, and Microsoft constituted the list's top five. Although the survey is comprehensive, it is deficient in measuring the actual monetary value attributable to innovation. Figure 7.5 shows how survey respondents measured the success of innovation. It is disappointing that only 30 percent indicated that they measure the actual ROI on innovation.

Creativity

Creativity, often considered the precursor to innovation, encompasses the creative experience, actions, and input of organizations. Measuring the creative spirit of employees may prove more difficult than measuring innovation. The employee suggestion system, a longtime measure of the creative processes of an organization, flourishes today in many organizations. Employees are rewarded for their suggestions if they are approved and implemented. Tracking the suggestion rates and benchmarking them against those of other

Figure 7.5. Measuring the Success of Innovation

Metric	Percentage of Respondents Using Metric
Overall revenue growth	56%
Percentage of sales from new products or services	50%
Customer satisfaction	47%
Return on investment in innovation	30%
Number of new products or services	30%
New product success ratio	20%
Higher prices	11%

Source: Adapted from McGregor, 2006, p. 63.

organizations is an important way to measure creative capability. Another measure that can be monitored is the number of new ideas. Formal feedback systems often generate creative suggestions that can lead to improved processes.

Some organizations measure the creative capabilities of employees by distributing inventories or instruments at meetings or training sessions. In other organizations, a range of statements about employee creativity is included in the annual employee feedback survey. Using a rating scale, employees agree or disagree with the statements. Comparing the ratings of groups of employees over time reflects the degree to which employees perceive improvement in creativity in the workplace. Having consistent and comparable measures is still a challenge. Other organizations may monitor the number, duration, and participation rate of creativity training programs. These methods illustrate the proliferation of creativity tools, programs, and activity in the last decade.

Example 3: Employee Attitudes

Employee Satisfaction

An important item monitored by most organizations is employee job satisfaction. Using feedback surveys, executives can monitor the degree to which employees are satisfied with their employer's policies, work environment, and supervision and leadership; with the work itself; and with other factors. A composite rating may be developed in order to provide an overall satisfaction value or an index for an organization, division, department, or region.

Although job satisfaction has always been an important factor in employee relations, in recent years it has taken on a new dimension because of the link between job satisfaction and other measures. The relationship between job satisfaction and the attraction and retention of employees is classic: firms with excellent ratings in job satisfaction have better success in attracting the most desirable employees. Organizations with job satisfaction ratings high enough that they are listed among the employers of choice or best places to work have gained a powerful recruiting tool. Recent heightened emphasis on the relationship between job satisfaction and employee retention has resulted from the reality that turnover and retention are now such critical issues. These relationships can now be easily worked out by using human capital management software featuring modules that calculate the correlation between turnover rates and job satisfaction scores for various job groups, divisions, and departments.

Job satisfaction has taken on new dimensions in connection with customer service. Dozens of applied research projects are beginning to show a high correlation between job satisfaction scores and customer satisfaction scores. Intuitively, one understands that a more satisfied employee is likely to provide more productive, friendly, and appropriate customer service. Likewise, a disgruntled employee will provide poor service. Research has established that job attitudes (job satisfaction) relate to customer impression (customer satisfaction), which relates to revenue growth (profits). Therefore, it follows that if employee attitudes improve, revenues will increase. These links, often referred to as a *service profit chain*, create a promising way to identify important relationships between attitudes within an organization and the profits that the organization earns.

Organizational Commitment

In recent years, organizational commitment (OC) measures have complemented or replaced job satisfaction measures. OC measures go beyond employee satisfaction to include the extent to which employees identify with an organization's goals, mission, philosophy, values, policies, and practices. The concept of involvement and commitment to the organization is key. OC often closely correlates with productivity and other performance improvement measures, whereas job satisfaction usually does not. OC is often measured in the same way as job satisfaction, using an attitude survey with a 5- or 7-point scale that is administered directly to employees. As organizational commitment scores (usually measured by a standard index) improve, a corresponding improvement in productivity should be seen.

Employee Engagement

A different twist on the OC measure is one that reflects employee engagement. Measures are taken that indicate the extent to which employees are actively engaged in the organization. Consider the case of the Royal Bank of Scotland Group (RBS). With more than 115,000 employees, RBS considered it a strategic imperative to measure the effectiveness of its investment in people and the impact of this investment on business performance. As a result, RBS built, validated, and introduced a human capital model that demonstrably links "people strategies" to performance (Bates, 2003).

RBS moved beyond monitoring employee satisfaction and commitment to measuring whether employees actively improved business results. The bank accomplished this by using an employee engagement model that assesses employees' likelihood of contributing to business profits. The model links separate elements of human resources (HR) information in a consistent way, then links them to key business indicators. The outputs enabled RBS to understand how to influence the bank's results through its workforce.

To test and validate its model, RBS's HR research and measurement team reviewed the array of survey instruments used in HR activities. The HR team decided to put the employee engagement model into practice in the processing and customer contact centers, where productivity measures related to customer service are very important. Using the amount of work processed as a throughput measure, the team found that productivity increased in tandem with engagement levels. They were also able to establish a correlation between increasing engagement and decreasing staff turnover.

Hundreds of organizations now use engagement data to understand the extent to which employees are engaged and how their engagement relates to productivity and turnover.

Example 4: Leadership

Leadership is perhaps the most difficult measure to address. On the surface, it would seem easy to measure the outcome, because effective leadership leads to an effective organization. However, putting a monetary value on the consequences of new leadership behavior is not as easy as it appears.

Leadership can (and usually does) determine the success or failure of an organization. Without appropriate leadership behaviors throughout an organization, resources can be misapplied or wasted, and opportunities can be missed. The news and literature are laced with examples of failed leadership at the top, as well as accounts of mismanagement of employees, shareholders, investors, and the public. Some of these high-profile failed leadership stories have been painful. At the same time, there are positive examples of leaders—for example, former General Electric CEO Jack Welch—who have earned extraordinary success at many levels of their organization over a sustained period. These leaders are often documented in books, articles, and lists of admiration. They clearly make a difference in their organization.

How can that difference be measured? Obviously, the ultimate measure of leadership is the overall success of an organization. Whenever overall measures of success have been achieved or surpassed, they are always attributed to great leadership, perhaps rightly. However, attempting to use overall success as the only measure of leadership is a cop-out in terms of accountability. Other measures must be in place to provide systemwide monitoring of leaders and leadership in an organization.

360° Feedback

Leadership can be measured in many different ways, the most common of which is known as 360° feedback. Here, a prescribed set of leadership behaviors desired in the organization is assessed by different sources to provide a composite of overall leadership capability and behavior. The sources often consist of the immediate manager of the leader being assessed, a colleague in the same area, the employees directly supervised by the leader, internal or external customers, and the leader's self-assessment. Combined, these assessments form a circle of influence (360°). The measure is basically an observation of behavior captured in a survey, often reported electronically. The practice of 360° feedback has been growing rapidly in the United States, Europe, and Asia as an important way to capture overall leadership behavior change. Because the consequences of behavior change are usually measured as business impact, leadership improvement should be linked to business performance in some way.

Leadership Inventories

Another way to measure leadership is to require the management team to participate in a variety of leadership inventories in which they assess themselves by responding to a series of leadership competency statements. The inventories reflect the extent to which a particular leadership style, a particular approach, or even success is in place. These inventories, though they were popular in the 1970s and 1980s, are now being replaced by the 360° feedback process in many organizations.

Leadership Perception

It is also useful to capture the quality of leadership from the perspective of employees. In some organizations, employees regularly rate the quality of their leadership. Top executives and middle managers are typically the subjects of this form of evaluation. The measure is usually taken in conjunction with the annual feedback survey, in the form of direct statements about the executive or immediate manager, with which respondents agree or disagree, using a 5-point scale. This type of survey attempts to measure how the followers in a particular situation perceive the quality, success, and appropriateness of the leadership exercised by their managers.

Business Impact

The outcomes of leadership development are clearly documented in many case studies involving ROI analysis. Of the thousands of studies conducted annually, leadership development ROI studies are at the top of the list of applications, not because conducting them is easier but because of the uncertainty and the unknown aspects of investing in leadership development.

Most leadership development will have an impact in a particular leader's area. Leadership development creates new skills that are applied on the job and produce improvements in the leader's work unit. These improvements can vary significantly from leader to leader and from unit to unit. The best way to evaluate a general leadership development program involving executives and leaders from a variety of areas is to calculate its monetary impact. When particular improvements are made, examining those improvements individually makes little sense. Examining the monetary value of each measure as a whole is more worthwhile. The measures are converted to monetary values using one of the methods discussed earlier in this book. The monetary values of the improvements for the first year are combined into a total value, which ultimately feeds into an ROI calculation. Leadership development programs aimed at improving leadership behavior and driving business improvement often yield a high payoff, with ROI values that range from 500 percent to 1,000 percent (Phillips and Schmidt, 2004). This high yield is primarily due to the multiplicative effect as leaders are developed and changes of behavior influence important measures within the leaders' teams.

Final Thoughts

It should be clear by now that intangible measures are crucial to gauging the success of a program. Although they may not carry the weight of measures expressed in monetary terms, they are nevertheless an important part of the overall evaluation. Intangible measures should be identified, explored, examined, and monitored for changes linked to programs. Collectively, they add a unique dimension to the program report because most if not all programs involve intangible variables. We have explored five common intangible measures in some detail in this chapter, but the fact is that the range of intangible measures is practically limitless.

References

Alden, J. "Measuring the 'Unmeasurable.'" *Performance Improvement*, May/June 2006, 45(5), 7.

Bates, S. *Linking People Measures to Strategy*. Research report R-1342-03-RR. New York: Conference Board, 2003.

Boulton, R., Libert, B., and Samek, S. *Cracking the Value Code*. New York: Harper-Business, 2000.

Brown, S. "Scientific Americans." *Fortune*, Sept. 20, 2004, p. 175.

Collins, J. *Good to Great and the Social Sector*. New York: HarperCollins, 2005.

Farris, P. W., Bendle, N. T., Pfeifer, P. E., and Ribstein, D. J. *Marketing Metrics: 50+ Metrics Every Executive Should Master*. Upper Saddle River, N.J.: Wharton School Publishing, 2006.

Kandybihn, A., and Kihn, M. "Raising Your Return on Innovation Investment." *Strategy + Business: Resilience Report*, May 11, 2004, no. 35, 1–12.

McGregor, J. "The World's Most Innovative Companies." *BusinessWeek*, Apr. 24, 2006, p. 63.

Phillips, J., and Schmidt, L. *The Leadership Scorecard*. Woburn, Mass.: Butterworth-Heinemann, 2004.

Santos, J., Doz, Y., and Williamson, P. "Is Your Innovation Process Global?" *MIT Sloan Management Review*, Summer 2004, 45(4), 31–37.

Schwartz, E. *Juice: The Creative Fuel That Drives World-Class Inventors*. Boston: Harvard Business School Press, 2004.

Index

About the Authors

Patricia Pulliam Phillips, Ph.D., is president of the ROI Institute, Inc., the leading source of ROI competency building, implementation support, networking, and research. She supports organizations in their efforts to build accountability into their training, human resources, and performance improvement programs with a primary focus on building accountability in public sector organizations. She helps organizations implement the ROI Methodology in countries around the world, including South Africa, Singapore, Japan, New Zealand, Australia, Italy, Turkey, France, Germany, Canada, and the United States.

In 1997, after a thirteen-year career in the electrical utility industry, she embraced the ROI Methodology by committing herself to ongoing research and practice. To this end, Phillips has implemented the ROI Methodology in private sector and public sector organizations. She has conducted ROI impact studies of programs in leadership development, sales, new-hire orientation, human performance improvement, K–12 educator development, National Board Certification mentoring for educators, and faculty fellowship. Phillips is currently expanding her interest in public sector accountability by applying the ROI Methodology in community- and faith-based initiatives.

Phillips teaches others to implement the ROI Methodology through the ROI certification process, as a facilitator for ASTD's

ROI and Measuring and Evaluating Learning workshops, and as an adjunct professor for graduate-level evaluation courses. She speaks on the topic of ROI at conferences such as ASTD's International Conference and Exposition and the International Society for Performance Improvement's International Conference.

Phillips's academic accomplishments include a master's degree in public and private management and a Ph.D. degree in international development. She is certified in ROI evaluation and has earned the designation of certified performance technologist (CPT) and certified professional in learning and performance (CPLP). She has authored a number of publications on the subject of accountability and ROI, including *Show Me the Money: How to Determine ROI in People, Projects, and Programs* (Berrett-Koehler, 2007); *The Value of Learning* (Pfeiffer, 2007); *Return on Investment (ROI) Basics* (ASTD, 2005); *Proving the Value of HR: How and Why to Measure ROI* (Society for Human Resource Management, 2005); *Make Training Evaluation Work* (ASTD, 2004); *The Bottomline on ROI* (Center for Effective Performance, 2002), which won the 2003 ISPI Award of Excellence; *ROI at Work* (ASTD, 2005); the ASTD In Action casebooks *Measuring Return on Investment,* Volume 3 (2001), *Measuring ROI in the Public Sector* (2002), and *Retaining Your Best Employees* (2002); the ASTD Infoline series, including *Planning and Using Evaluation Data* (2003), *Mastering ROI* (1998), and *Managing Evaluation Shortcuts* (2001); and *The Human Resources Scorecard: Measuring Return on Investment* (Butterworth-Heinemann, 2001). Phillips's work has been published in a variety of journals. She can be reached at patti@roiinstitute.net.

Holly Burkett, M.A., SPHR, CPT, is principal of Evaluation Works and has been a certified ROI professional (CRP) since 1997. As an internal and external consultant, she has more than eighteen years of experience assisting diverse public and private sector organizations to design and measure a wide range of evaluation processes, programs, and systems. Formerly with Apple Computer, she led the operation's first HRD impact studies. Editor-in-chief of ISPI's *Performance Improvement Journal* and a certified performance technologist (CPT), she is a frequent conference presenter, workshop leader, and author on performance measurement topics. Most recently, she coauthored *The ROI Fieldbook* (with Jack Phillips, Patricia Phillips, and Ron Stone, 2006). She earned her M.A. degree in human resources and organization development from the University of San Francisco and is currently pursuing doctoral studies in human capital development. She can be reached at burketth@earthlink.net.

Pfeiffer Publications Guide

This guide is designed to familiarize you with the various types of Pfeiffer publications. The formats section describes the various types of products that we publish; the methodologies section describes the many different ways that content might be provided within a product. We also provide a list of the topic areas in which we publish.

FORMATS

In addition to its extensive book-publishing program, Pfeiffer offers content in an array of formats, from fieldbooks for the practitioner to complete, ready-to-use training packages that support group learning.

FIELDBOOK Designed to provide information and guidance to practitioners in the midst of action. Most fieldbooks are companions to another, sometimes earlier, work, from which its ideas are derived; the fieldbook makes practical what was theoretical in the original text. Fieldbooks can certainly be read from cover to cover. More likely, though, you'll find yourself bouncing around following a particular theme, or dipping in as the mood, and the situation, dictate.

HANDBOOK A contributed volume of work on a single topic, comprising an eclectic mix of ideas, case studies, and best practices sourced by practitioners and experts in the field.

An editor or team of editors usually is appointed to seek out contributors and to evaluate content for relevance to the topic. Think of a handbook not as a ready-to-eat meal, but as a cookbook of ingredients that enables you to create the most fitting experience for the occasion.

RESOURCE Materials designed to support group learning. They come in many forms: a complete, ready-to-use exercise (such as a game); a comprehensive resource on one topic (such as conflict management) containing a variety of methods and approaches; or a collection of like-minded activities (such as icebreakers) on multiple subjects and situations.

TRAINING PACKAGE An entire, ready-to-use learning program that focuses on a particular topic or skill. All packages comprise a guide for the facilitator/trainer and a workbook for the participants. Some packages are supported with additional media—such as video—or learning aids, instruments, or other devices to help participants understand concepts or practice and develop skills.

- *Facilitator/trainer's guide* Contains an introduction to the program, advice on how to organize and facilitate the learning event, and step-by-step instructor notes. The guide also contains copies of presentation materials—handouts, presentations, and overhead designs, for example—used in the program.

- *Participant's workbook* Contains exercises and reading materials that support the learning goal and serves as a valuable reference and support guide for participants in the weeks and months that follow the learning event. Typically, each participant will require his or her own workbook.

ELECTRONIC CD-ROMs and web-based products transform static Pfeiffer content into dynamic, interactive experiences. Designed to take advantage of the searchability, automation, and ease-of-use that technology provides, our e-products bring convenience and immediate accessibility to your workspace.

METHODOLOGIES

CASE STUDY A presentation, in narrative form, of an actual event that has occurred inside an organization. Case studies are not prescriptive, nor are they used to prove a point; they are designed to develop critical analysis and decision-making skills. A case study has a specific time frame, specifies a sequence of events, is narrative in structure, and contains a plot structure—an issue (what should be/have been done?). Use case studies when the goal is to enable participants to apply previously learned theories to the circumstances in the case, decide what is pertinent, identify the real issues, decide what should have been done, and develop a plan of action.

ENERGIZER A short activity that develops readiness for the next session or learning event. Energizers are most commonly used after a break or lunch to stimulate or refocus the group. Many involve some form of physical activity, so they are a useful way to counter post-lunch lethargy. Other uses include transitioning from one topic to another, where "mental" distancing is important.

EXPERIENTIAL LEARNING ACTIVITY (ELA) A facilitator-led intervention that moves participants through the learning cycle from experience to application (also known as a Structured Experience). ELAs are carefully thought-out designs in which there is a definite learning purpose and intended outcome. Each step—everything that participants do during the activity—facilitates the accomplishment of the stated goal. Each ELA includes complete instructions for facilitating the intervention and a clear statement of goals, suggested group size and timing, materials required, an explanation of the process, and, where appropriate, possible variations to the activity. (For more detail on Experiential Learning Activities, see the Introduction to the *Reference Guide to Handbooks and Annuals*, 1999 edition, Pfeiffer, San Francisco.)

GAME A group activity that has the purpose of fostering team spirit and togetherness in addition to the achievement of a pre-stated goal. Usually contrived—undertaking a desert expedition, for example—this type of learning method offers an engaging means for participants to demonstrate and practice business and interpersonal skills. Games are effective for team building and personal development mainly because the goal is subordinate to the process—the means through which participants reach decisions, collaborate, communicate, and generate trust and understanding. Games often engage teams in "friendly" competition.

ICEBREAKER A (usually) short activity designed to help participants overcome initial anxiety in a training session and/or to acquaint the participants with one another. An icebreaker can be a fun activity or can be tied to specific topics or training goals. While a useful tool in itself, the icebreaker comes into its own in situations where tension or resistance exists within a group.

INSTRUMENT A device used to assess, appraise, evaluate, describe, classify, and summarize various aspects of human behavior. The term used to describe an instrument depends primarily on its format and purpose. These terms include survey, questionnaire, inventory, diagnostic, survey, and poll. Some uses of instruments include providing instrumental feedback to group members, studying here-and-now processes or functioning within a group, manipulating group composition, and evaluating outcomes of training and other interventions.

Instruments are popular in the training and HR field because, in general, more growth can occur if an individual is provided with a method for focusing specifically on his or her own behavior. Instruments also are used to obtain information that will serve as a basis for change and to assist in workforce planning efforts.

Paper-and-pencil tests still dominate the instrument landscape with a typical package comprising a facilitator's guide, which offers advice on administering the instrument and interpreting the collected data, and an initial set of instruments. Additional instruments are available separately. Pfeiffer, though, is investing heavily in e-instruments. Electronic instrumentation provides effortless distribution and, for larger groups particularly, offers advantages over paper-and-pencil tests in the time it takes to analyze data and provide feedback.

LECTURETTE A short talk that provides an explanation of a principle, model, or process that is pertinent to the participants' current learning needs. A lecturette is intended to establish a common language bond between the trainer and the participants by providing a mutual frame of reference. Use a lecturette as an introduction to a group activity or event, as an interjection during an event, or as a handout.

MODEL A graphic depiction of a system or process and the relationship among its elements. Models provide a frame of reference and something more tangible, and more easily remembered, than a verbal explanation. They also give participants something to "go on," enabling them to track their own progress as they experience the dynamics, processes, and relationships being depicted in the model.

ROLE PLAY A technique in which people assume a role in a situation/scenario: a customer service rep in an angry-customer exchange, for example. The way in which the role is approached is then discussed and feedback is offered. The role play is often repeated using a different approach and/or incorporating changes made based on feedback received. In other words, role playing is a spontaneous interaction involving realistic behavior under artificial (and safe) conditions.

SIMULATION A methodology for understanding the interrelationships among components of a system or process. Simulations differ from games in that they test or use a model that depicts or mirrors some aspect of reality in form, if not necessarily in content. Learning occurs by studying the effects of change on one or more factors of the model. Simulations are commonly used to test hypotheses about what happens in a system—often referred to as "what if?" analysis—or to examine best-case/worst-case scenarios.

THEORY A presentation of an idea from a conjectural perspective. Theories are useful because they encourage us to examine behavior and phenomena through a different lens.

TOPICS

The twin goals of providing effective and practical solutions for workforce training and organization development and meeting the educational needs of training and human resource professionals shape Pfeiffer's publishing program. Core topics include the following:

Leadership & Management

Communication & Presentation

Coaching & Mentoring

Training & Development

E-Learning

Teams & Collaboration

OD & Strategic Planning

Human Resources

Consulting

What will you find on pfeiffer.com?

• The best in workplace performance solutions for training and
  HR professionals

• Downloadable training tools, exercises, and content

• Web-exclusive offers

• Training tips, articles, and news

• Seamless on-line ordering

• Author guidelines, information on becoming a Pfeiffer Affiliate,
  and much more

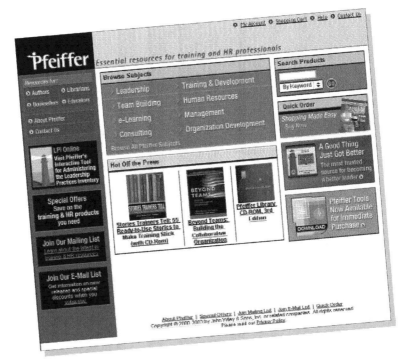

Discover more at www.pfeiffer.com

Measurement and Evaluation Series

Series Editors
Patricia Pulliam Phillips, Ph.D., and Jack J. Phillips, Ph.D.

A six-book set that provides a step-by-step system for planning, measuring, calculating, and communicating evaluation and Return-on-Investment for training and development, featuring:

- Detailed templates
- Complete plans
- Ready-to-use tools
- Real-world case examples

The M&E Series features:

1. *ROI Fundamentals: Why and When to Measure ROI*
   (978-0-7879-8716-9)
2. *Data Collection: Planning For and Collecting All Types of Data*
   (978-0-7879-8718-3)
3. *Isolation of Results: Defining the Impact of the Program*
   (978-0-7879-8719-0)
4. *Data Conversion: Calculating the Monetary Benefits*
   (978-0-7879-8720-6)
5. *Costs and ROI: Evaluating at the Ultimate Level*
   (978-0-7879-8721-3)
6. *Communication and Implementation: Sustaining the Practice*
   (978-0-7879-8722-0)

Plus, the *ROI in Action Casebook* (978-0-7879-8717-6) covers all the major workplace learning and performance applications, including Leadership Development, Sales Training, Performance Improvement, Technical Skills Training, Information Technology Training, Orientation and OJT, and Supervisor Training.

The **ROI Methodology** is a comprehensive measurement and evaluation process that collects six types of measures: Reaction, Satisfaction, and Planned Action; Learning; Application and Implementation; Business Impact; Return on Investment; and Intangible Measures. The process provides a step-by-step system for evaluation and planning, data collection, data analysis, and reporting. It is appropriate for the measurement and evaluation of *all* kinds of performance improvement programs and activities, including training and development, learning, human resources, coaching, meetings and events, consulting, and project management.

Special Offer from the ROI Institute

Send for your own ROI Process Model, an indispensable tool for implementing and presenting ROI in your organization. The ROI Institute is offering an exclusive gift to readers of The Measurement and Evaluation Series. This 11"×25" multicolor foldout shows the ROI Methodology flow model and the key issues surrounding the implementation of the ROI Methodology. This easy-to-understand overview of the ROI Methodology has proven invaluable to countless professionals when implementing the ROI Methodology. Please return this page or e-mail your information to the address below to receive your free foldout (a $6.00 value). Please check your area(s) of interest in ROI.

Please send me the ROI Process Model described in the book. I am interested in learning more about the following ROI materials and services:

☐ Workshops and briefing on ROI   ☐ ROI consulting services
☐ Books and support materials on ROI ☐ ROI Network information
☐ Certification in the ROI Methodology ☐ ROI benchmarking
☐ ROI software   ☐ ROI research

Name _____

Title _____

Organization _____

Address _____

Phone _____

E-mail Address _____

Functional area of interest:

☐ Learning and Development/Performance Improvement
☐ Human Resources/Human Capital
☐ Public Relations/Community Affairs/Government Relations
☐ Consulting
☐ Sales/Marketing
☐ Technology/IT Systems
☐ Project Management Solutions
☐ Quality/Six Sigma
☐ Operations/Methods/Engineering
☐ Research and Development/Innovations
☐ Finance/Compliance
☐ Logistics/Distribution/Supply Chain
☐ Public Policy Initiatives
☐ Social Programs
☐ Other (Please Specify) _____

Organizational Level

☐ executive   ☐ management ☐ consultant   ☐ specialist
☐ student   ☐ evaluator   ☐ researcher

Return this form or contact   The ROI Institute
                              P.O. Box 380637
                              Birmingham, AL 35238-0637

Or e-mail information to info@roiinstitute.net
Please allow four to six weeks for delivery.

Printed in the United States
By Bookmasters